ROYAL COURT

The Royal Court Theatre presents

THE PRIORY

by **Michael Wynne**

First performance at Royal Court Jerwood Theatre Downstairs, Sloane Square, London
on 19th November 2009.

THE PRIORY

by Michael Wynne

Cast in order of appearance
Kate **Jessica Hynes**
Daniel **Joseph Millson**
Ben **Alaistair Mackenzie**
Laura **Charlotte Riley**
Carl **Rupert Penry-Jones**
Rebecca **Rachael Stirling**
Adam **Nick Blood**

Director **Jeremy Herrin**
Designer **Robert Innes Hopkins**
Lighting Designer **Neil Austin**
Sound & Music Designer **Nick Powell**
Costume Designers **Robert Innes Hopkins, Iona Kenrick**
Casting Director **Amy Ball**
Assistant Director **Joe Murphy**
Production Manager **Paul Handley**
Stage Manager **Abi Coyle**
Deputy Stage Manager **Catherine Buffrey**
Assistant Stage Manager **Bryony Drury**
Stage Management Work Placement **Sophie Rubenstein**
Set built by **Miraculous Engineering & Rupert Blakely**
Set painted by **Kerry Jolson**

The Royal Court Theatre and Stage Management would like to thank the following for their help with this production: Apple Ltd, Bob (Alba Luggage), Colin Brown (The London Lighting Company), The Chelsea Gardener, Harriet Evans, Jon Fielding, Reverend Rob Gillion, Katy Harris, Oliver James, Emma Marsh, Nick Marston, Rosie Milne, Bill Prince, Gillian Reid, Dorothy Rowe, Sue Teller, Andrew Tuck, Louise Williams.

THE COMPANY

MICHAEL WYNNE (Writer)

FOR THE ROYAL COURT: The People are Friendly, The Knocky.

OTHER PLAYS INCLUDE: Tits/Teeth (National Youth Theatre/Soho Theatre); The Boy Who Left Home (ATC); Sell Out, Dirty Wonderland (Frantic Assembly).

TELEVISION INCLUDES: Substance, Eyes Down, UGetMe, Mayo, Grafters, Where The Heart Is, Don't Eat the Neighbours, As If, Sugar Rush.

FILM INCLUDES: My Summer of Love (co writer).

AWARDS INCLUDE: Meyer Whitworth Award - Best New Writer for The Knocky; Time Out Theatre Awards - Best Off West End Play for Sell Out; BAFTA - Best British Film Award for My Summer of Love; Evening Standard Film Awards - Best Screenplay for My Summer of Love.

NEIL AUSTIN (Lighting Designer)

FOR THE ROYAL COURT: Tusk Tusk, Flesh Wound, Trust.

OTHER THEATRE INCLUDES: The Observer, England People Very Nice, Mrs Affleck, Oedipus, Her Naked Skin, Afterlife, The Emperor Jones, Philistines, The Man of Mode, Thérèse Raquin, The Seafarer, Henry IV Parts 1 & 2, Fix Up, The Night Season, A Prayer for Owen Meany, The Walls, Further than the Furthest Thing (National); Hamlet (also Broadway), Madame de Sade, Twelfth Night (Donmar West End); Piaf (also Buenos Aires), Parade (also Los Angeles), John Gabriel Borkman, Don Juan in Soho, The Cryptogram, Frost/Nixon (also Broadway & US Tour), The Wild Duck, The Cosmonaut's Last Message to the Woman He Once Loved in the Former Soviet Union, Henry IV, World Music, After Miss Julie, Caligula (Donmar); King Lear, The Seagull, Much Ado About Nothing, Romeo & Juliet, King John, Julius Caesar, Two Gentleman of Verona (RSC); Mrs Klein, Judgment Day, The Homecoming, Marianne Dreams, Dying for it, Tom & Viv, Romance, Macbeth (Almeida); No Man's Land, Dealer's Choice, A Life in the Theatre, Japes (West End).

DANCE INCLUDES: Seven Deadly Sins (Royal Ballet); Pinocchio (ROH2); Highland Fling (UK Tour); Play Without Words (National/UK Tour/Moscow/Los Angeles); Les Liaisons Dangereuses (Tokyo/London).

AWARDS INCLUDE: 2008 Knight of Illumination Award for Parade.

NICK BLOOD (Adam)

THEATRE INCLUDES: Inches Apart (Theatre 503).

TELEVISION INCLUDES: Material Girl, The Bill.

Nick is co-founder of WE.BUY.GOLD. Theatre Company, winners of the Old Vic New Voices and Theatre 503 Award 2009.

JEREMY HERRIN (Director)

FOR THE ROYAL COURT: Tusk Tusk, The Vertical Hour, That Face (& Duke of York's).

OTHER THEATRE INCLUDES: Marble (Abbey, Dublin); The Family Reunion (Donmar); Blackbird (Market Theatre, Johannesburg); Statement of Regret (National); Sudden Collapses in Public Places, The Boy on the

Swing, Gathered Dust and Dead Skin, The Lovers, Our Kind of Fun, Toast, Dirty Nets, Smack Family Robinson, Attachments, From the Underworld, The Last Post, Personal Belongings, ne1, Knives in Hens (Live Theatre).

FOR THE ROYAL COURT, AS ASSISTANT DIRECTOR: My Night with Reg, Babies, Thyestes, The Kitchen.

FILM & TELEVISION INCLUDES: Linked, Dead Terry, Warmth, Cold Calling.

Jeremy is Deputy Artistic Director at the Royal Court.

ROBERT INNES HOPKINS (Designer)

FOR THE ROYAL COURT: Tusk Tusk, The Pain and the Itch, Redundant.

OTHER THEATRE INCLUDES: Wallenstein, Carousel (Chichester Festival Theatre); Marble (Abbey, Dublin); Dallas Sweetman (Canterbury Cathedral); Romeo & Juliet, Twelfth Night (Open Air Theatre, Regent's Park); The Member of the Wedding (Young Vic); Our Country's Good (Liverpool Playhouse).

OPERA INCLUDES: Xerxes (Stockholm Opera); Rape of Lucretia (Snape Maltings); Billy Budd (Santa Fe Opera); Carmen (Bolshoi); Lohengrin (Geneva Opera) Rigoletto (Lyric Opera, Chicago); Betrothal in a Monastery (Glyndebourne); Die Soldaten (Ruhr Triennale/Lincoln Center Festival.

AWARDS INCLUDE: Opernwelt Set Designer of the Year 2007 for Die Soldaten.

JESSICA HYNES (Kate)

FOR THE ROYAL COURT: The Night Heron.

OTHER THEATRE INCLUDES: The Norman Conquests (Old Vic/Broadway); Blithe Spirit (York Theatre Royal); Fiddler on the Roof, The Plough and the Stars, Brighton Rock (West Yorkshire Playhouse).

TELEVISION INCLUDES: Learners, Doctor Who, Pinochet in Suburbia, Miss Marple, Bob & Rose, Randall & Hopkirk, Spaced, People Like Us, The Royle Family, Midsomer Murders, Staying Alive, Asylum, Tears before Bedtime, House of Eliott.

FILM INCLUDES: Faintheart, Magicians, Son of Rambow, Harry Potter and the Order of the Phoenix, Four Last Songs, Confetti, Bridget Jones: The Edge of Reason, Shaun of the Dead, Pure, Tomorrow La Scala, Born Romantic, Swing Kids, The Baby of Macon.

ALASTAIR MACKENZIE (Ben)

THEATRE INCLUDES: The Gigli Concert (Assembly Rooms); Chain Play (Almeida); Four Dogs and a Bone (Etcetera); The Sorcerers' Apprentice (Citizens, Glasgow).

TELEVISION INCLUDES: The Mentalist, The Fall of Rome, Monarch of the Glen, Psychos, The Shell Seekers, Strange, The Brief, Death on the Nile, The Reichenbach Falls, Lewis, The Murdoch Mysteries.

FILM INCLUDES: The Last Great Wilderness, Man with a Movie Camera, New Town Killers, The Edge of Love, Boca a Boca, California Sunshine, Misadventures of Margaret, Monster Mutt.

JOSEPH MILLSON (Daniel)

FOR THE ROYAL COURT: Fear & Misery.

OTHER THEATRE INCLUDES: Judgment Day (Almeida); Every Good Boy Deserves Favour, Pillars of the Community (National); The Fairy Queen (Glyndebourne); Much Ado About Nothing, King John, The Dog in the Manger, House of Desires, Pedro The Great Pretender (RSC/West End); Hamlet (Stafford Gatehouse); Cinderella (Old Vic); The Seagull, Cold Meat Party (Manchester Royal Exchange); Richard II (Almagro/Ludlow); As You Like It (Peter Hall Co. UK & US Tour); The Lifted Veil (one man show); The Clearing, Mill on the Floss (Shared Experience); The Real Inspector Hound/Black Comedy (Donmar/West End); Gasping, The Talented Mr Ripley (Watford Palace); Monogamy (Riverside Studios); David Copperfield (Sheffield Crucible); The Fantasticks (Kings Head); Cinderella (Buxton); The Beaux Stratagem (Cannizaro Park); Four Nights in Knaresborough, Salad Days, The Rivals, The Dramatis, David Copperfield: The Musical, Loot (UK Tours).

TELEVISION INCLUDES: Campus, Enid, Ashes to Ashes, Survivors, Harley St, Midsomer Murders, Talk to Me, The Sarah Jane Adventures, New Tricks, Ghost Squad, The Romantics, Macbeth, Holby City, Eastenders, In Exile, Dressing For Breakfast, Doctors, Peak Practice.

FILM INCLUDES: Telstar, Casino Royale, Abraham's Point, Devil's Bridge.

RADIO INCLUDES: The Fairy Queen, The Threepenny Opera, Maud, Brief Lives, Cheri, The Tractate Middoth, One Man On A Stage, Steinbeck in Avalon, Monogamy, The Voice of Angels, Maud in Black.

JOE MURPHY (Assistant Director)

THEATRE INCLUDES: 2nd May 1997 Wrap-around (nabokov at The Bush); Service, Building Site (Miniaturists at Arcola); After, Come on Over (Tristan Bates); The Things That Never Grew in the Garden (Hampstead Start Night); Normal (Cockpit); Julius Caesar, Esme-Tales (Edinburgh Fringe); South Pacific (Northcott).

AS ASSISTANT DIRECTOR: 2nd May 1997 (The Bush); Fixer (High Tide Festival); Purgatory (Arcola); Girls and Dolls (Old Red Lion); He Said... (The Bush).

Joe is Artistic Director of nobokov theatre company.

RUPERT PENRY-JONES (Carl)

THEATRE INCLUDES: Power, Chips with Everything (National); The Play About the Baby (Almeida); Les Liaisons Dangereuses (Bristol Old Vic); Don Carlos, Timon of Athens (RSC); The Paper Husband, Sweet Panic (Hampstead).

TELEVISION INCLUDES: The 39 Steps, Whitechapel, Burn Up, Spooks, Joe's Palace, Persuasion, Krakatoa, Casanova, Poirot, Cambridge Spies, North Square, The Student Prince, Jane Eyre, French & Saunders, Absolutely Fabulous, Fatherland.

FILM INCLUDES: Red Tails, Match Point, Charlotte Gray, The Four Feathers, Still Crazy, Virtual Sexuality, Hilary & Jackie, Food of Love.

NICK POWELL (Sound & Music Designer)

FOR THE ROYAL COURT: Relocated, The Vertical Hour, The Wonderful World Of Dissocia (with National Theatre of Scotland & Tour).

OTHER THEATRE INCLUDES: The Drunks (RSC); Tito Andronico (Animalario, Madrid); Panic (Improbable); The Family Reunion (Donmar); Bonheur (Comedie Francais); God in Ruins (RSC); Marat-Sade, Urtain (Spanish National Theatre/ Animalario); Realism (Edinburgh International Festival); (co-created) The Wolves in the Walls (National Theatre of Scotland & Improbable).

FILM INCLUDES: Beneath The Veil, Death in Gaza.

Nick has worked extensively with companies including the National Theatre, Paines Plough and Improbable as well as twelve shows with Suspect Culture which he founded with Graham Eatough and David Greig. Nick toured and recorded with McAlmont & Butler (Chrysalis), Strangelove (EMI Records), Astrid (Nude Records) and Witness (Island Records). He is one half of Oskar, who have performed live scores for three Prada fashion shows in Milan, exhibited installations at the V&A and the CCA Glagsow as well as producing two albums, Air Conditioning and 2009's LP:2. For more information see www.oskaronline.com.

CHARLOTTE RILEY (Laura)

THEATRE INCLUDES: The Cherry Orchard (Chichester Festival Theatre).

TELEVISION INCLUDES: Miss Marple, The Forgotten Fallen, Foyle's War, The Take, Wuthering Heights, George Gently, Holby City, Dis/connected, Grown Ups.

FILM INCLUDES: Easy Virtue.

RACHAEL STIRLING (Rebecca)

THEATRE INCLUDES: Pygmalion (Hong Kong Festival); Uncle Vanya, Taming of the Shrew (Wilton's Music Hall); Look Back in Anger (Theatre Royal Bath); Tamburlaine (Bristol Old Vic); Theatre of Blood (National); Anna in the Tropics (Hampstead); A Woman of No Importance (West End); Helpless (Donmar); Dancing at Lughhnasa (Arts Theatre); Othello (Royal Theatre, Glasgow/Bloomsbury Theatre).

TELEVISION INCLUDES: Minder, Boy Meets Girls, Lewis, The Haunting of Toby Jugg, Riot at the Rite, Miss Marple, The Quest III, Poirot, Tipping the Velvet, Bait, Othello, In The Beginning.

FILM INCLUDES: Apollo & The Continents, Centurion, The Truth, Framed, Redemption Road, Triumph of Love, Another Life, Maybe Baby, Complicity, Still Crazy.

RADIO INCLUDES: Hold Back The Night, The Pallisers.

New Season 2010

Jerwood Theatre Downstairs

11 February – 13 March

off the endz
By Bola Agbaje

9 April – 22 May

posh
By Laura Wade

11 June – 24 July

sucker punch
By Roy Williams

Jerwood Theatre Upstairs

17 February – 20 March

disconnect
By Anupama Chandrasekhar

31 March – 1 May

the empire
By DC Moore

20 May – 19 June

ingredient x
By Nick Grosso

14 July – 14 August

spur of the moment
By Anya Reiss

020 7565 5000
www.royalcourttheatre.com

THE ENGLISH STAGE COMPANY
AT THE ROYAL COURT

'For me the theatre is really a religion or way of life. You must decide what you feel the world is about and what you want to say about it, so that everything in the theatre you work in is saying the same thing ... A theatre must have a recognisable attitude. It will have one, whether you like it or not.'

George Devine, first artistic director of the English Stage Company: notes for an unwritten book.

photo: Stephen Cummiskey

As Britain's leading national company dedicated to new work, the Royal Court Theatre produces new plays of the highest quality, working with writers from all backgrounds, and addressing the problems and possibilities of our time.

"The Royal Court has been at the centre of British cultural life for the past 50 years, an engine room for new writing and constantly transforming the theatrical culture." Stephen Daldry

Since its foundation in 1956, the Royal Court has presented premieres by almost every leading contemporary British playwright, from John Osborne's Look Back in Anger to Caryl Churchill's A Number and Tom Stoppard's Rock 'n' Roll. Just some of the other writers to have chosen the Royal Court to premiere their work include Edward Albee, John Arden, Richard Bean, Samuel Beckett, Edward Bond, Leo Butler, Jez Butterworth, Martin Crimp, Ariel Dorfman, Stella Feehily, Christopher Hampton, David Hare, Eugène Ionesco, Ann Jellicoe, Terry Johnson, Sarah Kane, David Mamet, Martin McDonagh, Conor McPherson, Joe Penhall, Lucy Prebble, Mark Ravenhill, Simon Stephens, Wole Soyinka, Polly Stenham, David Storey, Debbie Tucker Green, Arnold Wesker and Roy Williams.

"It is risky to miss a production there." Financial Times

In addition to its full-scale productions, the Royal Court also facilitates international work at a grass roots level, developing exchanges which bring young writers to Britain and sending British writers, actors and directors to work with artists around the world. The research and play development arm of the Royal Court Theatre, The Studio, finds the most exciting and diverse range of new voices in the UK. The Studio runs play-writing groups including the Young Writers Programme, Critical Mass for black, Asian and minority ethnic writers and the biennial Young Writers Festival. For further information, go to www.royalcourttheatre.com/ywp.

"Yes, the Royal Court is on a roll. Yes, Dominic Cooke has just the genius and kick that this venue needs... It's fist-bitingly exciting." Independent

PROGRAMME SUPPORTERS

The Royal Court (English Stage Company Ltd) receives its principal funding from Arts Council England, London. It is also supported financially by a wide range of private companies, charitable and public bodies, and earns the remainder of its income from the box office and its own trading activities.

The Genesis Foundation supports the Royal Court's work with International Playwrights.

The Jerwood Charitable Foundation supports new plays by new playwrights through the Jerwood New Playwrights series.

The Artistic Director's Chair is supported by a lead grant from The Peter Jay Sharp Foundation, contributing to the activities of the Artistic Director's office. Over the past ten years the BBC has supported the Gerald Chapman Fund for directors.

ROYAL COURT DEVELOPMENT ADVOCATES
John Ayton
Elizabeth Bandeen
Tim Blythe
Anthony Burton
Sindy Caplan
Cas Donald
Allie Esiri
Celeste Fenichel
Anoushka Healy
Stephen Marquardt
Emma Marsh (Vice Chair)
Mark Robinson
William Russell (Chair)
Deborah Shaw Marquardt
Nick Wheeler
Daniel Winterfeldt

PUBLIC FUNDING
Arts Council England, London
British Council

CHARITABLE DONATIONS
American Friends of the Royal Court Theatre
Anthony Burton
Gerald Chapman Fund
Credit Suisse First Boston Foundation*
Cowley Charitable Trust
The Edmond de Rothschild Foundation*
Do Well Foundation Ltd*
The D'Oyly Carte Charitable Trust
Frederick Loewe Foundation*
Genesis Foundation
Jerwood Charitable Foundation
John Thaw Foundation
John Lyon's Charity
The Laura Pels Foundation*
The Martin Bowley Charitable Trust
The Patchwork Charitable Foundation*
Paul Hamlyn Foundation
Jerome Robbins Foundation*
Rose Foundation

Royal College of Psychiatrists
The Peter Jay Sharp Foundation*
Sobell Foundation

CORPORATE SUPPORTERS & SPONSORS
BBC
Bloomberg
Ecosse Films
Hugo Boss

BUSINESS BENEFACTORS & MEMBERS
Grey London
Lazard
Merrill Lynch
Vanity Fair

AMERICAN FRIENDS OF THE ROYAL COURT
Rachel Bail
Francis Finlay
Amanda Foreman & Jonathan Barton
Imelda Liddiard
Stephen McGruder & Angeline Goreau
Alexandra Munroe & Robert Rosenkranz
Ben Rauch & Margaret Scott
David & Andrea Thurm
Amanda Vaill & Tom Stewart
Monica Voldstad
Franklin Wallis

INDIVIDUAL MEMBERS

ICE-BREAKERS
Act IV
Anonymous
Ossi and Paul Burger
Mrs Helena Butler
Lindsey Carlon
Cynthia Corbett
Virginia Finegold
Charlotte & Nick Fraser
Mark & Rebecca Goldbart
The David Hyman Charitable Trust
David Lanch
Watcyn Lewis

David Marks QC
Nicola McFarland
Janet & Michael Orr
Pauline Pinder
Mr & Mrs William Poeton
Wendy Press
The Really Useful Group
Lois Sieff OBE
Gail Steele
Nick & Louise Steidl

GROUND-BREAKERS
Anonymous
Moira Andreae
Jane Attias*
Elizabeth & Adam Bandeen
Philip Blackwell
Stan & Val Bond
Mrs D H Brett
Sindy & Jonathan Caplan
Mr & Mrs Gavin Casey
Kay Ellen Consolver
Clyde Cooper
Andrew & Amanda Cryer
Robyn M Durie
Denise Dumas
Allie Esiri
Celeste & Peter Fenichel
John Garfield
Lydia & Manfred Gorvy
Richard & Marcia Grand*
Reade & Elizabeth Griffith
Don & Sue Guiney
Douglas & Mary Hampson
Nicholas Josefowitz
David P Kaskel & Christopher A Teano
Peter & Maria Kellner*
Mrs Joan Kingsley & Mr Philip Kingsley
Mr & Mrs Pawel Kisielewski
Rosemary Leith
Kathryn Ludlow
Emma Marsh
Barbara Minto
Murray North
Gavin & Ann Neath
William Plapinger & Cassie Murray*
Mr & Mrs Tim Reid
Mark Robinson
Paul Robinson
Paul & Jill Ruddock
William & Hilary Russell

Sally & Anthony Salz
Jenny Sheridan
Anthony Simpson
Brian D. Smith
Samantha & Darren Smith
Sheila Steinberg
Carl & Martha Tack
Nick & Chrissie Wheeler
Katherine & Michael Yates

BOUNDARY-BREAKERS
John & Annoushka Ayton
Katie Bradford
Tim Fosberry
Rosanna Laurence

MOVER-SHAKERS
Anonymous
Cas & Philip Donald
Duncan Matthews QC
The David & Elaine Potter Charitable Foundation
Ian & Carol Sellars

HISTORY-MAKERS
Jack & Linda Keenan*
Miles Morland
Jan & Michael Topham

MAJOR DONORS
Rob & Siri Cope
Daniel & Joanna Friel
Deborah & Stephen Marquardt
Lady Sainsbury of Turville
NoraLee & Jon Sedmak*
The Williams Charitable Trust

*Supporters of the American Friends of the Royal Court (AFRCT)

FOR THE ROYAL COURT

Royal Court Theatre, Sloane Square, London SW1W 8AS
Tel: 020 7565 5050 Fax: 020 7565 5001
info@royalcourttheatre.com, www.royalcourttheatre.com

Artistic Director **Dominic Cooke**
Deputy Artistic Director **Jeremy Herrin**
Associate Director **Sacha Wares**+*
Artistic Associate **Emily McLaughlin**
Diversity Associate **Ola Animashawun***
Education Associate **Lynne Gagliano***
PA to the Artistic Director **Victoria Reilly**

Literary Manager **Ruth Little**
Senior Reader **Nicola Wass****
Literary Assistant **Marcelo Dos Santos**

Associate Director International **Elyse Dodgson**
International Administrator **Chris James**
International Assistant **William Drew**

Studio Administrator **Clare McQuillan**
Writers' Tutor **Leo Butler***

Casting Director **Amy Ball**
Casting Assistant **Lotte Hines**

Head of Production **Paul Handley**
JTU Production Manager **Tariq Rifaat**
Production Administrator **Sarah Davies**
Head of Lighting **Matt Drury**
Lighting Deputy **Stephen Andrews**
Lighting Assistant **Katie Pitt**
Acting Lighting Assistant **Emily Ellsworth**
Lighting Board Operator **Tom Lightbody**
Head of Stage **Steven Stickler**
Stage Deputy **Duncan Russell**
Stage Chargehand **Lee Crimmen**
Chargehand Carpenter **Richard Martin**
Head of Sound **David McSeveney**
Sound Deputy **Alex Caplen**
Head of Costume **Iona Kenrick**
Costume Deputy **Jackie Orton**
Wardrobe Assistant **Pam Anson**

Executive Director **Kate Horton**
Head of Finance & Administration **Helen Perryer**
Planning Administrator **Davina Shah**
Senior Finance & Administration Officer **Martin Wheeler**
Finance Officer **Rachel Harrison***
Finance & Administration Assistant **Tessa Rivers**

Head of Communications **Kym Bartlett**
Marketing Manager **Becky Wootton**
Press & Public Affairs Officer **Anna Evans**
Press Consultant **Nancy Poole**
Audience Development Officer **Gemma Frayne**
Sales Manager **Kevin West**
Deputy Sales Manager **Daniel Alicandro**
Box Office Sales Assistants **Cheryl Gallagher,
Shane Hough, Ciara O'Toole**

Head of Development **Gaby Styles**
Senior Development Manager **Hannah Clifford**
Trusts & Foundations Manager **Khalila Hassouna**
Development Officer **Lucy Buxton**
Development Assistant **Penny Saward**
Development Intern **Morwenna Johnson**
US Fundraising Counsel **Tim Runion**

Theatre Manager **Bobbie Stokes**
Deputy Theatre Manager **Daniel O'Neill**
Front of House Manager **Siobhan Lightfoot**
Duty Manager **Stuart Grey***
Bar & Food Manager **Baljinder Kalirai**
Head Chef **Charlie Brookman**
Events Manager **Joanna Ostrom**
Bookshop Manager **Simon David**
Assistant Bookshop Manager **Edin Suljic***
Bookshop Assistant **Vanessa Hammick** *
Customer Service Assistant **Deidre Lennon***
Stage Door/Reception **Simon David***, **Paul Lovegrove,
Tyrone Lucas**

Thanks to all of our box office assistants, ushers and bar staff.

+ Sacha Wares' post is supported by the BBC through the
Gerald Chapman Fund.

** The post of Senior Reader is supported by NoraLee & Jon
Sedmak through the American Friends of the Royal Court Theatre.

* Part-time.

ENGLISH STAGE COMPANY

President
Dame Joan Plowright CBE

Honorary Council
Sir Richard Eyre CBE
Alan Grieve CBE
Martin Paisner CBE

Council
Chairman **Anthony Burton**
Vice Chairman **Graham Devlin**

Members
Jennette Arnold
Judy Daish
Sir David Green KCMG
Joyce Hytner OBE
Stephen Jeffreys
Wasfi Kani OBE
Phyllida Lloyd
James Midgley
Sophie Okonedo
Alan Rickman
Anita Scott
Katharine Viner
Stewart Wood

Michael Wynne
The Priory

faber and faber

First published in 2009
by Faber and Faber Limited
74–77 Great Russell Street
London WC1B 3DA

Typeset by Country Setting, Kingsdown, Kent CT14 8ES
Printed in England by CPI Bookmarque, Croydon, Surrey

All rights reserved
© Michael Wynne, 2009

The right of Michael Wynne to be identified as author
of this work has been asserted in accordance with Section 77
of the Copyright, Designs and Patents Act 1988

All rights whatsoever in this work are strictly reserved.
Applications for permission for any use whatsoever,
including performance rights, must be made in advance, prior
to any such proposed use, to Independent Talent Group Limited,
Oxford House, 76 Oxford Street, London W1D 1BS.
No performance may be given unless a licence has first
been obtained

*This book is sold subject to the condition that it shall not,
by way of trade or otherwise, be lent, resold, hired out or
otherwise circulated without the publisher's prior consent
in any form of binding or cover other than that in which
it is published and without a similar condition including
this condition being imposed on the subsequent purchaser*

A CIP record for this book
is available from the British Library

ISBN 978-0-571-25483-5

2 4 6 8 10 9 7 5 3 1

For Johanna Wynne

Acknowledgements

I would like to thank Debra Oswald, Paul Keating,
Michael McCoy, April De Angelis, Jeremy Herrin,
Dominic Cooke and Ruth Little
for their invaluable help with this play.

Michael

Characters

Kate

Daniel

Ben

Laura

Carl

Rebecca

Adam

THE PRIORY

Act One

SCENE ONE

*Mid-afternoon in the large living room of an isolated
country house.*

*An impressive place, very stylishly decorated with a
mixture of modern and traditional furniture. Lots of
wood panelling everywhere. A big heavy door on the
back wall, up a couple of steps. Windows either side.
Trees can be seen through the windows. Two doorways
on the right side, one to the kitchen, the other to the
bedrooms. A doorway on the other side leads to a
bathroom, library and other rooms. A large fireplace on
the left with sofas and coffee table in front of it. A dining
table on the right. A cabinet with bottles and glasses on it.
A bookcase filled with books and retro board games.*

*The room has a slightly religious air with a couple of
small stained-glass windows and a church-like ceiling.
A large stag's head dominates one wall.*

*Kate sits on the sofa reading a book from the bookshelf.
A cup of tea and half-read newspapers next to her. She is
dressed casually. She takes a sip of tea and turns the page
of her book. She looks very relaxed. She looks sharply
across the room as she thinks she hears a floorboard
creak. She looks around, waiting for another noise, but
nothing comes. She seems quite distracted. She goes back
to her book.*

*A hooded face appears at the left-hand window and
peers through. It's not clear enough to make out who it is.
Then quickly disappears out of sight.*

*There's a knock on the knocker at the door. Kate's
slightly startled. She gets up excitedly to answer it.*

Kate Thank God.

She opens the big heavy door wide open. There's no one there.

Hello?

Kate steps out and looks right and left. There's no one to be seen.

Is this one of you messing about?

No answer.

Oh, don't do this. Lou? Mini?

She looks again either side. She's quite unnerved now.

Daniel, is this you?

Kate looks at the door knocker. She lifts it up and lets it fall. It's quite loose. She convinces herself it must have been the wind. She shuts the door and locks it. And bolts it.

She comes down the steps and takes in the rest of the room. She goes back to the sofa and picks up her book but immediately puts it back down on the coffee table. She's rattled and not sure what to do. She heads over to have a look in the kitchen but decides to go off towards the bedrooms.

A Man in a black hood peeps round the kitchen door. He sees that no one's about and comes into the living room. He creeps about, trying not to make any noise. He takes in the room, looking around. He picks up Kate's book and moves it to the dining table. As he does he bangs his shin on the coffee table and he lets out a scream.

Man Ow!

He covers his mouth, though it's too late as he's already made a noise. He's not sure what to do. He runs off through the doorway leading to the library.

Kate comes back into the living room to see where the noise came from. She's breathing fast and becoming more anxious.

Kate Hello? Is there someone . . . I know it's one of you lot. This isn't funny now.

No answer. She takes out her mobile phone and looks at it. There's no signal. She holds it up around the room trying to get a signal but has no luck. She passes the coffee table and sees that her book is gone.

Oh no.

She then notices it on the dining table.

Oh no.

She looks back to where she left it.

Please no.

She tries to convince herself that she moved it, half re-enacting a mime of how she moved it on the way out.

That's it.

But she's really not convinced. She picks the book up, holding it tight so it can't be moved again. She goes off to the kitchen, quite determined.
The Man comes back into the room. He sees that the book has gone. He's not sure what to do. He's now getting unnerved himself as there's no one about. He moves to go back into the kitchen but changes his mind and goes off towards the bedrooms.
Kate comes back on quickly, armed with a large, heavy fire poker.

Come on then.

She looks round at all the possible doors and out through the windows but there's no one about. She stands strong in the middle of the room with her weapon ready for whatever's going to happen. It's all too much. She goes off through the doorway leading to the library.

The Man just misses Kate as he comes back in quickly from the bedrooms. He looks around, getting more frustrated and unnerved.

Man Where . . . ?

He goes off to look for Kate in the kitchen.
The room stays empty for a moment. Pause.
Kate and the Man both come back on at exactly the same time and both clock each other. They both let out a loud scream. Kate's brandishing her weapon.
But then she realises it's Daniel.

Kate What the fuck are you doing?

Daniel What the fuck are you doing?

Kate Creeping round here, scaring the shit out of me.

Daniel What are you doing stalking the house with a big metal poker?

Kate How was I meant to know who it was?

Daniel I was just messing about. Who else was it going to be?

Kate It could have been anyone. We're in the middle of bloody nowhere. Anyone could just walk up here and no one would know.

Daniel Are you a bit on edge?

Kate (*manic*) No, not at all. I'm absolutely fine. (*Slightly calmer but still fraught.*) Well, maybe a bit on edge. It's this place. I've only been here five hours and I've never been so terrified in my whole life. We're nowhere near anyone else. In the middle of a wood. There's no noise

14

whatsoever. Which you'd think would be nice, that's just what I wanted. Get away, peace and quiet. But my brain's in overdrive that there's some escaped lunatic on the loose and he breaks in and nobody knows. And you all turn up and find me hung, drawn and quartered.

Daniel Nice.

Kate And every now and again there's a creak or a rumble or a branch tapping at the window. Who lets their trees grow so they can tap on the window like some long pointy finger? Why would you do that? Or some other sound from the house that you can't quite put your finger on. It's absolutely terrifying. And then there'll just be deathly silence. Which is so loud I can't hear anything else. If you know what I mean. I like big cities, where there's continual noise. Where you can hear your neighbour farting in the bath or snoring through the wall next door. So you aren't left with your own crazy thoughts. I complain about all the continual noise but I'm really missing it. I'll be fine now you're here.

Daniel And what were you going to do with that?

Kate I don't know. I just thought, I have to protect myself.

Daniel Do you want to put it down now?

Kate Oh yeah. (*She puts the poker down.*) And we're cut off from everything up here. There's no phone, you can't get a signal . . .

Daniel takes out his mobile phone and looks at it.

Daniel There must be.

He walks round the room trying to get a signal.

Kate I've tried every room, I couldn't get anything.

Daniel I take it there's no broadband?

Kate What do you reckon? Have you brought your laptop?

Daniel I just might need to check emails and stuff.

Kate You're on holiday. It's New Year, no one will be working now. The whole idea of this is to get away from everything.

Daniel I know, I know. (*He looks around.*) There's no telly is there?

Kate No.

Daniel Of course there isn't. It's great. It's going to be great. Let's have a drink?

Daniel surreptitiously continues to move round the room looking for a signal as they talk.

Kate I'll put the kettle on.

Daniel I've just sat on one of those trains that stops at every station in the country. I need a drink.

Kate I wasn't going to drink.

Daniel It's New Year's Eve. You're having a party.

Kate It's not really a party.

Daniel (*sarcastic*) This is going to be fun.

Kate I don't want to start the New Year with a hangover.

Daniel's still looking for a signal.

Will you stop looking? You're not going to find a signal.

Daniel puts his phone in his pocket.

I suppose a drink or two won't do us any harm. Gin and tonic?

Daniel Perfect.

Kate starts making the drinks. She gets out two tumblers.

Kate How did you get in?

Daniel The kitchen door was unlocked.

Kate It wasn't?

Daniel That's what people do in the countryside. You don't need to lock your doors round here.

Kate Ice and tonic. I think we should.

She goes off to the kitchen. Daniel looks round the room.

Daniel If you insist. We should have come together.

Kate (*off*) I wanted to get everything ready.

Daniel And pick the best room.

Kate (*off*) No. Not really.

She comes back on with tonic and an ice bucket.

I've locked it, just to be safe. I've made this into the bar here.

Kate goes over to a sideboard which has bottles and glasses laid out. She makes two gin and tonics.

I have decided where everyone is going to go. I've put little name tags on each door. You've got a really nice four-poster in the medieval porch bedroom.

Daniel I do like a medieval porch. I love that it's called The Priory. It's like our own little rehab.

Kate The monks all lived in this bit. You can see the remains of the chapel next door.

Daniel To think this place used to be full of mad monks all walking round in silence with big black cloaks on. I'm not surprised you were shitting yourself.

Kate I'm fine now.

Daniel So is this going to be like a spiritual retreat?

Kate Yeah, we're going to be the monks. It'll be a time of peace, quiet and contemplation. I might even do some yoga.

Kate's finished making the drinks. She hands Daniel his drink.

Daniel Maybe a few drinks first.

Kate Cheers.

Daniel Cheers.

They clink glasses and drink.

Kate That's better. I'm glad you're here, I can relax.

Daniel I was expecting some fusty old house. It's really fancy.

Kate It's run by this couple who used to do club nights years ago. They've got a few houses dotted about. It's big business.

Daniel Is it going to work out really expensive?

Kate No, Matthew had already paid half as a deposit.

Daniel That's one good thing he did.

Kate We'll just sort out the rest. It so knows who it's aimed at. We could have had a chef cook for us. But I know that's your department. You tell them what drink you want and they fill up the fridge. I'm sure they'd sort out drugs if you asked.

Daniel D'you reckon?

Kate You know it's not going to be that sort of thing.

Daniel I know, I know.

Kate There's a pool table, board games, there's even a dressing-up box. I might not tell anyone about that.

Kate sits down on the sofa. Daniel strolls round the room as they talk.

There's loads of food and drink. Got the lamb and everything you asked for for dinner. There's tons of books, guide books, walks we can do. There's a seal sanctuary nearby somewhere.

Daniel A really calm New Year, no pressure.

Kate A few friends. People we like. No craziness. The days of a big blowout are over. I normally hate New Year. All that fuss and hysteria for one moment.

Daniel I like it. You can look back at the year and –

Kate Wish it never happened?

Daniel Or look forward to the new one with a fresh start.

Kate I've got a really good feeling about next year. It's all going to come together. It can't be worse than this year. Have you recovered from Christmas?

Daniel Only just. That's the last time I go home for a family Christmas. So dysfunctional. We all can't stand each other but pretend we want to be there. Never again. Next year we should do something. I don't know how you ended up on your own.

Kate It was fine.

Daniel No one should be alone at Christmas.

Kate I had a nice time. Just did what I wanted to do. It was only when I was watching a film on Christmas Day and there was a little message along the bottom of the screen saying, 'Are you alone? Depressed? If you are call . . .' Well, I wasn't, but I am now. Had a little cry.

Well, quite a big one. Even looking at myself crying in the mirror, getting off on the drama of it all. Then I just drank red wine and ate cheese. So much cheese you wouldn't believe it. Took a sleeping tablet, went to bed. All good. Christmas over.

Daniel I think I might go away next year. Somewhere really hot with no families. (*He finds the guest book on the side and flicks through.*) Here's the guest book.

Kate I went to church on Christmas Day.

Daniel What?

Kate I went for a walk and I passed this church, thought I'd go in and light a candle for my mum.

Daniel Ah.

Kate There was a service going on, so I stayed. And I really enjoyed it. Sitting in this beautiful building, listening to a few good stories. Singing carols at the top of my voice. I could remember all the words. There was a real sense of community, they all knew each other. All coming together for something, and it's not about shopping or money or getting drunk.

Daniel Get you.

Kate Just to take some time and try and think good thoughts. I felt so happy. For a moment.

Daniel You're not going to get all religious, are you?

Kate I think religion could be the answer. Apparently people who have a faith are a lot happier.

Daniel Are you going to find God?

Kate I don't know. I like the idea of having a faith, something else. The whole believing in God part is a bit of a sticking point. But I'm sure I can work round that.

Daniel Oh look. (*He reads.*) 'We think we saw a ghost of a monk tonight. There was a black hooded figure in the kitchen. We all hid . . .'

Kate It doesn't say that.

Daniel Look.

Kate reads. She closes the book and puts it away.

Kate It'll be someone messing about. It's not real.

Daniel Is everyone else on their way?

Kate I hope so. I said any time after three. Lou and Mini should be here soon.

Daniel I thought it wasn't going to be 'that sort of thing'.

Kate They're really calming down now and I think they might be serious this time. Lou's not meant to drink since her liver failure.

Daniel Believe it when I see it. I bumped into Mini at the end of the summer. She'd just come back from Ibiza where she didn't go to bed for five days. I don't know how she does it. All that partying and still managing to run Children's BBC.

Kate I've told them what this'll be like and they're up for a quiet one.

Daniel We're not going to spend the whole time talking about when we used to take drugs and have fun, pretending that we're much happier now we're not doing any of that stuff.

Kate No, no.

Daniel And Carl *is* coming? On his own?

Kate Oh God, yeah. Rebecca won't want to leave the kids. And I couldn't be in the same house as her for a weekend.

Daniel She doesn't mind him coming here?

Kate I think she's doing something with her mother and she knows he can't stand her.

Daniel I saw her with the kids the other Sunday morning on Columbia Road. And she introduced me as 'Uncle Daniel'. I said, 'I'm not their uncle,' but she said, 'The children have lots of gay uncles.' She has to make some reference to my sexuality every time she sees me.

Kate Stupid cow.

Daniel I'm a real uncle to my brother's kids. I don't need to be some funny gay uncle to those two charmless little blonde things. Have you seen their kids lately? They just stood there and stared at me like the Midwich Cuckoos. Then the oldest one said, 'Mummy's won a Bafta.' And then said, 'Have you won any awards?' She's four. Don't even get me started on their names.

Kate And Ben's coming.

Daniel Benjamin?

Daniel joins Kate on the sofa.

Kate Yeah, I bumped into him and it was really great to see him. I think he's changed. He seemed much humbler.

Daniel Everything wasn't 'fantastic' and 'amazing'?

Kate No. There was some light and shade, some colour, for the first time in years. He's single . . .

Daniel Never.

Kate He said he's found it really hard but he now thinks it's the best thing that ever happened to him.

Daniel Of course he does.

Kate We had such a lovely chat, was like the Ben we first knew was back.

Daniel He is a laugh. All the old gang back together.

Kate He texted this morning to say he's definitely coming and could he bring a friend.

Daniel You don't mind?

Kate I'm really easy. People can come and go, do whatever they want. It's such a big house.

Daniel I'd be quite happy to just have the place to ourselves.

Kate It's great, isn't it?

Two figures walk past the window.

Daniel (*slightly surprised*) There's someone outside.

Kate Don't say it like that.

There's a knock at the door. Kate jumps slightly.

It'll be Lou and Mini.

She jumps up and opens the door. She sees it's Ben.

Oh Ben, come on in. So glad you could make it.

Ben steps inside with Laura. They are both dressed very stylishly, in the latest designer clothes. They look like the perfect couple.

Ben Wow. What an amazing place.

Laura Amazing.

Ben I love it.

Laura So do I.

Ben Hiya. You look great. Thanks for asking us.

He gives Kate a kiss. Daniel joins them.

(*To Daniel.*) Hello, you.

Daniel Benjamin. Good to see you. It's been ages.

They give each other a hug.

Ben This is Laura.

Laura Don't tell me. Kate. And Daniel?

Kate Yeah.

Daniel Yeah.

Laura kisses Kate enthusiastically.

Laura Hello.

Kate Hiya.

Laura kisses Daniel.

Laura Hello.

Daniel Hi.

Laura It's great to meet you. I've heard so much about you.

Kate Have you now?

Laura Ben's told me everything.

Ben Not quite.

Ben goes outside to get the bags.

Laura I just know we're going to have a great time together.

Kate Oh right. Good.

Ben brings in three heavy bags from outside.

Whose are these?

Ben Not mine.

Laura Just a couple of things.

Ben (*going back out*) Just get mine.

Kate How long are you planning on staying?

Laura I didn't know what to bring and I thought I should have a few looks.

Ben brings in a tiny holdall.

Ah, cute little baby bag.

Ben closes the door behind him.

Ben This place is amazing.

Laura Amazing. This is what grown-up people do.

Ben The way they've converted it. Done such a great job.

Laura It's a bit spooky, coming through those woods.

Kate Please don't say it's spooky.

Daniel She's a bit oversensitive about that. It's haunted by a mad monk.

Kate No, it's not.

Laura If I get scared will you look after me, baby?

Ben Of course, baby.

Laura You promise?

Ben I promise.

Laura Cross your heart and hope to die?

Ben I cross my heart and hope –

Kate I think he'll be there for you.

Ben How much do you think a place like this'd be worth?

Kate I hadn't thought about that.

Laura You'd be talking . . . a lot of money. A lot.

Kate I'll show you your room.

Daniel Don't you want a drink? We're on gin and tonics.

Ben That'd be great.

Kate Oh, okay. Laura?

Laura Have you got any Ribena?

Kate I don't think so. Cranberry juice?

Laura Perfect.

Kate goes off to the kitchen.

Ben We've got some exciting news.

Laura Are you going to tell them?

Ben I thought you said we were.

Laura We did. I'm just too excited.

Ben So am I.

Laura I can't say it.

Ben Neither can I.

Kate comes back in with a cranberry juice.

Daniel Please put us out of our misery.

Ben We're engaged.

Laura To be married.

Daniel Oh.

Kate What?

Ben Isn't it great?

Daniel Yeah, it's . . . really great.

Ben We could have our wedding here.

Laura It'd be perfect. But what about that castle I've got my heart set on?

Ben Oh yeah, it's got to be the castle.

Daniel So have you and . . .

Kate Laura.

Daniel Laura known each other long? I didn't even think you were going out with anyone.

Ben I wasn't.

Laura He wasn't.

Ben Till yesterday.

Laura We met at a party yesterday. The most amazing party.

Ben And just clicked. We've been inseparable ever since.

Laura I can't leave his side. I never want to be apart from him.

Daniel You met yesterday and now you're getting married? Wow.

Ben You know when you meet someone and it just clicks?

Laura You know from that minute you're going to spend the rest of your lives together?

Daniel No, not really.

Kate You're asking the wrong people.

Kate has made the drinks. She hands them over.

Laura Oh, thank you. I was sorry to hear about you and your boyfriend splitting up.

Kate Oh it's fine. Seems ages ago now.

Laura But it takes a long time to get over something like that . . .

Kate I suppose it can do . . .

Laura I was dumped once. It nearly destroyed me. Took to my bed and that was it. I thought I'll never find anyone else, but I did. And you know what, you will too. You'll find someone.

Kate D'you think so?

Laura I know so.

Kate Oh well, fingers crossed.

Laura You've got to get back out there. You're not getting any younger and all the good men get snapped up.

Kate . . .

Laura What moisturiser do you use?

Kate I just . . .

Laura Your pores are quite open, bit greasy. I'll give you a facial while we're here.

Kate Oh, thanks.

Ben That's so sweet of you. Laura works at the beauty spa at Harvey Nicks.

Laura (*to Daniel*) And I just know us two are going to get along brilliantly.

Daniel Yeah?

Ben She couldn't wait to meet you.

Laura Ben had told me about you. That you were gay. The gay one. But I knew, when I saw you. I knew. I can tell. I can always tell. And as soon as you opened your mouth I knew for sure.

Daniel Right.

Laura I love the gays. Well gay men. Not so much lesbians, they're a bit scary for me. If there's a party, I'll find the gays and I'll be in the corner having a laugh with them all night. They're a scream. They're always gorgeous, really trendy and the best dancers. And they're so rude. Always talking about sex and what you get up to. I was in this gay club the other week. I go to gay clubs on my own sometimes 'cause I just know I'll make a million friends and have a great time. Anyway, I'd lost my new friend, Jason, this gorgeous Australian hairdresser. Didn't know where he'd gone. Then he reappears and I'm like, 'Where've you been?' And he's like, 'I've just been sucking someone off in the toilet.' And then he's straight back on the dance floor. He didn't even know his name. All he knew was that he was Jewish. I sometimes wish I was gay. A gay man. Not that I'd be sucking off Jews in the toilets. It's not my sort of thing. I'm not good in cramped spaces and I've got a terrible gag reflex. I bet you love being gay, don't you?

Daniel Oh yeah, love it. Can't get enough of it. It's one of things I'm best at, being gay.

Laura You're hilarious.

Kate So . . .

Laura When Ben said we were coming here one of the first things I asked was, 'Are there going to be any gays there?' Thank God there is. Not that I don't mind everyone else. It's just it's not a party without a gay or two. (*To Ben.*) I love your friends.

Ben Isn't she wonderful?

Kate Yeah, great. Let me show you where you are.

Ben We'll find it. We'll explore.

Kate I've put a little label on the door. Second on the left.

Laura This is so exciting.

Ben picks up all the bags.
Laura heads through the upper left doorway.

(*Off.*) It is a bit spooky. Come and hold my hand, baby.

Ben Coming, baby. You don't mind me bringing Laura, do you?

Kate No. No. No. The more the merrier. It's cool.

Ben She's the most incredible woman I've ever met. So positive. I know we're going to be really happy together.

Laura comes back out.

Laura It's too scary down there.

Ben Don't worry, I'm here now.

They both go off towards the bedrooms.
Daniel looks towards Kate.

Kate Don't.

Daniel (*sarcastic*) Ben's really changed, hasn't he?

Kate I must have caught him on an off day. It's fine, it's a big house. She's harmless enough. And when everyone else is here their constant pawing at each other won't bother me.

Daniel Is it just we're too cynical and can't handle seeing other people happy?

Kate thinks for a second. Laura screams with laughter down the corridor.

Kate Probably, yeah. You've got a friend for life there in Laura.

Daniel Let's look at this kitchen.

Daniel heads off to the kitchen. Kate looks in a mirror.

Kate Do I look really that rough?

Kate is left alone. She starts to make herself another drink.

A knock at the door. Kate is startled slightly.
She opens the door. Carl is standing there.

Oh, it's you.

Carl Oh sorry. Shall I go?

Kate No, no. I thought you'd be someone else. Come in, come in.

Carl steps inside. He's carrying a box of champagne in his hands with a bag over his shoulder. She gives him a big hug and kiss.

How was it getting away? Was it a nightmare? I'm so glad you're here.

Carl I've got a surprise.

Kate What?

Rebecca steps into view. She's got a bag and a box of food.

Rebecca Surprise!

Kate Rebecca. You're here.

Rebecca I'm here.

Rebecca comes inside, putting down the box and bag.

Kate It's so good to see you.

She gives Rebecca a hug and a kiss.

Rebecca You too.

Kate Oh my God. Rebecca's here.

Carl I know.

Kate What a lovely surprise.

Rebecca You don't know how much we need this. I've baked a chocolate cake and some muffins. Gorgeous muffins, you'll love them.

Kate Oh, thanks.

Carl takes in the room.

Carl Now look at this. It's like Westminster Abbey.

Kate (*to Rebecca*) I thought you'd be looking after the kids.

Rebecca My mum said she'd babysit and I thought why not.

Carl The Ice Maiden's never offered before.

Rebecca This'll be the first proper night I've been away from them.

Kate They'll be fine.

Rebecca I'm more worried about her than them. I'll just give her a call, check she's okay.

Rebecca takes her mobile phone out.

Kate There's no reception in here.

Rebecca You're joking? What if something happens and my mum needs to contact me?

Carl The whole point of you coming was to get a break and your mum knows what she's doing, sort of.

Rebecca And anyway, I don't want to be one of those boring people who just talks about their kids all the time. That's the last thing I'm going to say about them. So, where's the drink? Where's the drugs?

Kate Well . . .

Rebecca I imagine these places are hard to get. Carl was telling me you and Matthew had booked it.

Carl Did you have to say that?

Rebecca It's not a secret, is it?

Kate Oh yeah. We booked it in the spring. Thought it'd be a nice way to end off the year. Little did I know.

Rebecca And you were going to come here with all his friends?

Kate I could have cancelled, it's not the sort of thing I'd naturally do but . . . I thought, I'll spend it with my friends instead. Catch up.

Carl (*he finds the pile of board games*) Buckaroo, Ker-Plunk, Guess Who . . . This is great.

Rebecca How are you?

Kate Fine, fine. Did you find it alright?

Carl We got a bit lost. She kept turning off . . .

Rebecca She? Who's she?

Carl Rebecca kept turning off the satnav.

Rebecca It was a fuckin' nightmare. The voice was doing my head in. It sent us all over the place. Through streams and everything.

Carl That was because you kept turning it off. It was losing its bearings.

Rebecca 'Turn around. Turn around.' We could have just used a map but Carl has to use one of his toys.

Carl You could have just slept. I don't know why you had to stay awake to irritate me.

Rebecca Piss off.

Carl You piss off.

Daniel comes through with his phone in his hand.

Daniel I nearly got a signal in there, but then it went. (*He sees Carl.*) Hey, Carl.

Carl Alright, mate, how you doing?

They give each other a hug.

Daniel I'm good, thanks.

Daniel sees Rebecca.

Oh my God, Rebecca.

Rebecca Daniel.

Daniel What a surprise.

Kate Isn't it?

Daniel Hiya.

They kiss.

Rebecca God, the last time I saw Daniel was on Columbia Road early one Sunday morning. I'd been up since six with the kids and he hasn't been to bed yet, on his way home from a sex club.

Daniel I hadn't been to a sex club. I've never been to a sex club.

Rebecca You know what I mean. It's just funny, there's me with my boring children and you're still doing all that. Out there having fun.

Daniel That was the only time I'd been out all night all year.

Rebecca Okay, I'm not your mother.

Carl I need a drink. Where shall we start?

Kate What would you like from the bar?

Carl Whisky and Coke.

Rebecca Vodka tonic for me please.

*Kate makes the drinks. Rebecca looks round.
An awkward pause.*

Carl So . . . how was your Christmas?

Daniel Good. Good, yeah.

Rebecca Ours was really great. It was the first year the kids knew what was going on, well mainly Clemmie. I think Archie will appreciate it next year. We decorated the house top to bottom, lights, tree, the lot. It was beautiful. Felt really magical. Tell them about Clemmie on Christmas Eve?

Carl They won't want to hear about this.

Daniel No, go on.

Carl She got into a right state about what food to leave out. So we spent most of Christmas Eve making, from scratch, a vegetable curry for Father Christmas and a mango fruit smoothie for Rud . . .

Rebecca You've missed out the bit about why she . . .

Carl Oh, because everyone would be leaving mince pies, whisky and carrots. She thought they'd want something else to eat.

Rebecca And the bit . . .

Carl Why don't you just tell it?

Rebecca And she wanted them to have a balanced diet and make sure they got five-a-day fruit and vegetables. Hence the veggie curry and the fruit smoothie.

Daniel I see.

Rebecca (*to Kate*) How was yours?

Kate Nice. Quiet, relaxing. Just what I needed.

Rebecca (*to Daniel*) What did you do?

Daniel I went home to my family.

Rebecca It's all about family, isn't it.

Daniel Oh, yeah.

Carl We really are in the middle of nowhere.

Rebecca It is a bit gothic, isn't it, bit creepy.

Kate If another person says that I'm going home.

Rebecca What's through here?

Rebecca goes through to the kitchen. Daniel follows.

Daniel (*off*) This is my domain. Check this out . . .

Kate and Carl are left alone.

Carl It's very impressive.

Kate . . .

Carl There's some history here.

Kate Hmm.

Carl This a real fire?

Kate Yeah. We'll light it later.

Carl What's through here?

Kate There's a bathroom, a library with a pool table . . .

Carl I'm sorry.

Kate It's fine.

Carl I didn't know she was coming. It was a last-minute thing.

Kate . . .

Carl She wanted it to be a surprise.

Kate It certainly is that.

Rebecca and Daniel come back through.

Rebecca It's incredible. How old is this place?

Kate Some of it's medieval but most of it was added on in Georgian times, I think. There's a guide book somewhere.

She finishes pouring the drinks and hands them over.

Here we are.

Carl and Rebecca take big swigs, almost knocking them back in one.

Carl I so need this.

Rebecca spots a half-read Observer *newspaper on the sofa.*

Rebecca Oh you've got a paper. (*She finds the reviews section.*) I couldn't get a copy. Apparently we're in here somewhere . . . What to look out for next year. (*She finds the page.*) Here we are. TV, *The Ark*. This years big-budget sci-fi drama for all the family. From the team that brought you *Cruel Earth*. Don't miss it.' Oh God, that's brilliant. You have to watch it, the special effects are amazing. I'm so proud of it.

Kate I'll look out for it.

Rebecca And there's meant to be . . . Here it is . . . *My Brother's War*. It's this amazing three-parter we've done about the Holocaust.

Daniel Great.

Rebecca It's really classy. It's by this incredible new writer, Jacob Horowitz. Only twenty-two, just left Cambridge. He's written this and he's got another two things with us. Just churns them out. 'Should clean up at all the awards.'

Carl (*taking the paper off her*) And who wrote this? What a surprise. Nicholas Hopkins. She went to school with him.

Rebecca That's got nothing to do with it.

Carl He hasn't even seen them. How can he recommend them?

Rebecca He knows our work. Knows it'll be good.

Carl You told me he's never seen any of your stuff.

Rebecca No, I didn't.

Daniel Things are going well, then?

Rebecca Bit too well, just got no time, you know what it's like, but mustn't complain. (*To Kate.*) Now, I want to hear all about your new book. Carl says you've got one coming out next year. And it's not short stories this time?

Kate Yeah, yeah. I thought I'd try and write a whole book.

Rebecca When's it out?

Kate We're still sorting out dates.

Rebecca Can't wait. I love your work. I still love that book of short stories you wrote after college about childhood. I would have loved to have been a writer.

Kate You still could be.

Rebecca Maybe I'll give it a go. When I've burnt myself out. And do you still do the stuff in the women's prison?

Kate Yeah, teach literacy couple of days a week at Holloway.

Rebecca That's so admirable. Teaching adults to read and write. It must change their lives.

Kate It can do, yeah.

Rebecca I need to do some charity work. (*To Daniel.*) And I hear you're doing really well now. Working on what will be London's tallest building.

Daniel Yeah, ours is one of the only ones still going ahead.

Carl Who else is coming?

Daniel Ben's already here with his fiancée.

Carl He hasn't got back with the Norwegian one? He told me –

Daniel This is a new one. He only met her yesterday.

Carl Right.

Kate Lou and Mini are on their way.

Carl Brilliant. Rebecca's terrified of those two.

Rebecca No, I'm not. What about David Chandler? Is he coming?

Kate No, I don't really see him any more.

Rebecca He's doing so well. Isn't he off in Hollywood now, doing films?

Kate I wouldn't know.

Rebecca He's such a lovely man. And his wife Miriam. Amazing interior designer. They're a real power couple now.

Carl A bit like us.

A sharp scream from Laura down the hall.

Daniel What was that?

Rebecca finishes her drink and picks up her bag.

Rebecca (*to Carl*) Let's dump our stuff.

Carl Where are we?

Kate Third on the left. I'll let you sort yourselves out. There's a tag with 'Carl' on the door. Hope you like it.

Rebecca and Carl go off to their room.
Kate is silent, deep in thought. Pause.

Daniel Do we have to be 'on' all weekend? Is she going to talk about work the whole time?

Kate doesn't answer.

It's not that bad, it'll be fun. We'll stick together. At least there's some sport now. Did you know she was coming?

Kate No.

Daniel Shall we just leave them all to it? Drive off?

Kate Thank God Lou and Mini are on their way.

Laura screams from down the hallway.
Carl comes out.

What's going on down there?

Carl Ben's future wife is freaked out by something.

Daniel goes back into the kitchen.

They're all swapping rooms. She's going into the attic room we were meant to be in.

Kate They can't swap rooms.

Carl Why not?

Kate It doesn't matter.

Carl I can tell them not to move.

Kate I just put us in rooms next to each other.

Carl She might only stay for one day and go back tomorrow.

Kate She can stay as long as she wants. I'm here with my friends, that's what this is all about.

Carl Don't be . . .

He reaches out to touch her.

Kate I knew I shouldn't have done this.

Rebecca comes into the room.

Rebecca She's hysterical. She needs someone to throw a bucket of water over her or slap her. Shall we form a queue? God, she's annoying.

Kate What's happening?

Rebecca She's moved into the attic where's there's no windows. She thought she saw someone outside.

Kate Like who?

Rebecca She said there was someone hanging about. Watching us.

Kate I don't think you'd get anyone up here.

Carl Maybe it was a local farmer or something.

Rebecca We're nowhere near anything. Someone could murder us all and no one would know.

Kate Please don't say that.

Rebecca Those sort of things do happen. There was this French girl at my school whose whole family were murdered one night by this escaped lunatic. He went through the house, room to room, and shot each one. She was shot in the arm and only survived by playing dead. She lay there for an hour with her dead mum's body on top of her while he sat in the same room smoking a whole packet of cigarettes. And then shot himself in the face.

Kate I can't believe you just told me that.

Carl Don't let Ben's girlfriend hear you.

Laura appears out of the doorway. She's wearing a completely different outfit.

Laura I heard every word.

She starts breathing heavily. Ben follows her.

Ben Thanks, Rebecca.

Rebecca I was only messing about. Of course it didn't happen.

Laura's breathing gets more laboured.

Ben It's alright now.

Laura Okay, baby.

Ben I'm here, baby. Nothing's going to happen to you while I'm here. Just sit down, we'll get you some water.

Laura sits on the sofa. Daniel comes in with a tray of light food.

Daniel Here we go. (*He sees Laura.*) Oh my God.

Kate Is she alright?

Ben I think it's a little panic attack.

Kate Have you had one before?

She shakes her head.

Rebecca It's this place that's brought it on. (*She looks at the food.*) This looks nice.

Daniel goes off to the kitchen.

Carl Shouldn't she breathe into a paper bag or something?

Rebecca I've got a plastic bag. Though she might suffocate.

Carl She's not going to put it over her head, is she?

Ben takes some pills out of his pocket and hands Laura one. She continues to breathe heavily.

Ben Here, take this.

Kate What is it?

Ben It's just a Valium.

Carl You've got Valium? Great.

Daniel comes back in with a glass of water. He hands it to Laura.

Rebecca You actually carry them round with you?

Ben I just happened to have them in my pocket. I don't know why.

Carl I love Valium. They're great with a drink. Take the edge off.

Laura Are you sure?

Ben It'll be fine.

Laura I'd rather not.

Carl If you don't want it, I'll have it.

Ben Go on.

Laura reluctantly takes the Valium.

That should help.

Carl Where d'you get them from?

Ben I know a dealer who does them. Valium, sleepers, anything.

Carl (*to Rebecca*) We should get his number.

Rebecca I can't remember the last time I had a good night's sleep.

Laura continues to breathe heavily in the background as they all get caught up in the discussion.

Carl We got a load when we went to Vietnam on holiday. Bought hundreds. I was gutted when they ran out.

Rebecca Tell me about it.

Carl My doctor gives me Zopiclone for sleeping. They're alright, but he'll only give me twelve.

Ben I don't like the metallic aftertaste.

Carl They're not strong enough. You have to take two to really paralyse you.

Daniel You used to be able to get these great ones over the counter in France, but they've stopped doing them.

Carl Limovan. Can't get them anywhere now. I tried the internet but they were duds. Think they were laxatives.

Kate You know what's meant to be really good? Rohypnol. The date-rape drug.

Carl I've heard that.

Daniel I went out for a works drink the other week and all the young secretaries were covering the top of their Bacardi Breezer bottles with their thumbs in case their drink was spiked and they were raped.

Kate Chance'd be a fine thing.

Daniel What about Xanax?

Rebecca Now you're talking.

Ben Amazing.

Kate Perfect on a long flight.

Carl Or a Wednesday night, for a midweek moment.

Rebecca I love anything with codeine in it.

44

Kate Oh yeah.

Laura's breathing calms down.

Ben You alright, baby?

Laura He was at the window. He stared at me.

Rebecca You sure it wasn't your reflection?

Ben She's not stupid.

Laura He was all dressed in black with a big hood up.

Kate Like a monk?

Laura Just like a monk.

Daniel Or the Grim Reaper?

Kate Oh God.

Daniel I suppose it's better he was outside than inside.

Kate Can we make sure all the doors are locked?

Rebecca Are you serious?

Kate Just in case.

Carl It was probably just a lost rambler.

Laura I feel okay now.

Ben That's good, baby.

He kisses her and they start snogging.

Daniel Oh my God.

Kate That'll take her mind off it.

*An awkward moment as they carry on kissing.
Everyone else doesn't know what to do.*

Daniel Here's some nibbles to tide us over.

Kate Oh great.

Daniel goes back out. They all go over to the table, help themselves.

Carl I'm starving.

Kate Hmm, lovely.

Ben and Laura stop kissing.

Thank God.

Laura I love you.

Ben I love you.

They make their way over to the others.

Kate (*to Laura*) Weren't you wearing something different earlier?

Laura Yeah, that was my travelling outfit. For . . .

Kate Travelling? Do you have a different outfit for each activity? What's this one?

Laura This is hanging out. Pre-dinner. Casual.

Kate Right.

Rebecca (*to Ben*) And where've you been lately? The man with the best job in the world.

Laura I know. Getting paid to go on holiday.

Ben Just come back from Dotonbori in Osaka.

Carl Haven't a clue where that is.

Ben Got the most amazing psychedelic nightlife, like one long acid trip. And before that I did a piece about Harajuku . . .

Carl You're making these up.

Ben In Tokyo. The maddest fashion you've ever seen. Amazing.

Laura He's going to take me on his next trip, as his assistant.

Ben I'm reviewing this incredible new five-star hotel in São Paulo. I'll sneak you in my bag.

Laura I'm only tiny.

Daniel brings out a bottle of champagne and a tray with champagne glasses on it.

Carl This is more like it.

Everyone takes a glass.

Laura Have you got any more juice?

Daniel Don't you want . . .

Ben Laura doesn't drink.

Rebecca Oh, why's that?

Carl (*under his breath*) For fuck's sake.

Laura It's no big deal. Just don't like the taste.

Daniel rushes off to the kitchen. Pause.

Kate Well, thanks for coming. The others should be here soon.

Ben It's great you got us all together. I can't remember the last time.

Rebecca Thank God Matthew dumped you so you could come here with all your friends instead of his.

Carl Rebecca.

Daniel comes back in with a glass of juice for Laura.

Laura You're an angel.

Rebecca Did I go too far?

Carl Yeah.

Kate It's fine. I got that it was a compliment in a sort of fucked-up way.

Rebecca Sorry. Here's to Kate . . .

She raises her glass. They all follow.

All Kate.

Rebecca And not to Matthew.

Carl Have you got any consideration for anyone else? Can't you just keep your big mouth shut?

Rebecca Oh, fuck you.

Laura Please don't argue.

Silence. Pause.

Daniel So what's the plan for tonight?

Kate Okay, here's what I was thinking. We'll hang out, have a few drinks. Have dinner. Daniel's going to cook.

Ben He's a great cook.

Laura Gays always are.

Daniel So, dinner about nine. We're having lamb. Are there any veggies?

Laura timidly puts her hand up.

And a roasted vegetable thing for Laura.

Laura That's so sweet.

Kate And then afterwards . . .

Rebecca We'll get the party going.

Ben I've brought a load of dance music. Old tunes we'll all know.

Rebecca I really need a good boogie.

Ben This is the perfect place for a party. We can turn the music right up.

Kate Let's just see what happens.

Laura I love New Year. This is going to be the best New Year's ever. I always wanted to know the sort of people who all went away together to big houses in the country.

Ben And now you do.

Kate I've got the bread and coal and stuff.

Ben What's that?

Kate It's . . .

Rebecca First footing. At midnight a young, good-looking, dark-haired male . . . one of you will have to do . . . comes into the house with some bread, coal, money and salt.

Ben Why?

Kate It's just a tradition. I like traditions, rituals. I think they're important.

Rebecca It's meant to bring good fortune to the house, whoever lives here. But seeing as none of us live here it doesn't quite make sense.

Kate I thought it'd be nice.

Daniel Yeah, let's do it.

Ben Why bread and coal and . . . ?

Kate I don't know.

Rebecca They're all symbols of wealth, apparently. It's about celebrating wealth and asking for more.

Laura Sounds like a good way to start the year.

Kate I'm not sure, I didn't know it was about that.

Ben Who doesn't want more wealth?

Kate I just don't want to start the New Year thinking of money. Anyway, it's not all about twelve o'clock.

Laura Oh yes it is.

Kate Well, we're here for a few days, it's about taking some time out. It doesn't have to be crazy at midnight.

Laura (*to Carl*) I'm sure I've met you before.

Carl Yeah?

Rebecca You haven't met him.

Carl She might have.

Ben Maybe you've seen him in something.

Laura Of course, you're an actor.

Ben What was that great film you were in?

Carl *Kingfisher Blue*. It was this indie thing . . .

Rebecca She won't have seen it.

Laura shakes her head.

Daniel He's done a lot of theatre.

Laura I don't really go the theatre.

Ben Or that police series.

Rebecca Just do the line.

Carl No. I was in a few episodes of . . .

Rebecca You know you want to.

Ben Go on.

Carl 'Wake up and smell the coffee.'

Laura Oh my God. It's you off those coffee adverts. Oh my God, you're famous.

Carl No, not really.

Laura Do you know loads of famous people?

Carl A few.

Laura Who? Who?

Kate Leave him alone, he's getting all embarrassed.

Rebecca No, he's not. He loves it. Can't get enough of it.

Kate Anyone want a top-up?

Ben Yes, please.

Kate tops up glasses.

Laura What are you in now?

Carl Got a few things in the pipeline, can't really say.

Laura You'll have to let me know when you're next going to be on the telly. I wish I had friends like you. You're all really successful, aren't you?

Rebecca I think successful people attract each other.

Laura The law of attraction.

Ben Oh yeah.

Rebecca No one wants to be associated with failure.

Kate It depends what you class as success.

Rebecca We don't really want for anything. We've all got good lives, good jobs, lovely children, some of us . . .

Daniel Are you a success if you've got children?

Rebecca It's an achievement.

Kate Who wants a proper look round? There's a library and pool table, a bowling alley . . .

Carl Why would monks build a bowling alley?

Kate It's just a long thin corridor with some skittles in it. Don't get too excited.

Laura (*to Rebecca*) And you and Carl are married, but Carl used to go out with Kate?

Rebecca Years and years ago when they were at college.

Laura And you're all such good friends now. It's so grown-up.

Ben and Laura head towards the doorway leading to the library.

Ben Down here?

Ben and Laura go through the doorway. He starts tickling her. She laughs.

Laura (*off*) Oh stop it. Oh, not in there, that's the toilet . . .

Rebecca Let's have a tournament.

Carl I'm not playing if you're going to get all competitive.

Rebecca What's the point in playing otherwise?

Rebecca and Carl go down the corridor.

Daniel I'd better start making dinner.

A mobile phone pings.

What's that?

Kate That's my phone.

Daniel You got a signal? How have you got a signal?

Kate puts down her glass. She takes her phone out of her bag and checks it.

Kate I've got a text message. And full signal. Oh, I did have, it's gone. (*She reads excitedly.*) It's Lou.

Daniel takes out his phone and checks for a signal. He stands where Kate's bag was.

Daniel Where was your phone?

Kate Oh. (*Reading.*) 'We're not gonna make it now. Going to a party at Shoreditch House. Might try and come tomorrow. See how twatted we are. Have a great one.' Oh, wonderful. And all written in teenage text speak. She's written great G-R-number eight.

Daniel That's a shame. Call them, tell them to come? If you can find another signal.

Kate I don't want to speak to them. If all they can do is send a text message. Do they know how much trouble I've gone to? Shoreditch fuckin' House.

Daniel They still might come.

Kate It's fine. Who needs them? It'll be great just us lot. Won't it?

Daniel I'd better get cracking with the cooking.

Kate D'you want a hand?

Daniel I'll get going on my own. I'll give you a shout . . .

Kate Okay.

Daniel goes off to the kitchen.
Kate isn't quite sure what to do. She looks over to the doorway leading to the library and bowling alley.

Rebecca (*off*) Strike!

And a cheer goes up.
She moves to join them. She'll need her drink. She goes to pick up her champagne glass but grabs it

awkwardly and knocks it smashing on the floor. It should almost look like an accident by the actress.

Kate Shit.

She picks up the broken bits of glass. She's clearly on edge. She cuts her finger on one of the pieces of glass.

Fuck.

Blood dribbles down her finger. She gets a tissue out of her bag and wraps it round her cut finger. She then takes the section of the Observer *Rebecca was reading and lays it on the floor. She methodically places the broken bits of glass in the newspaper.*

As she does a face in a black hood appears at the window looking in. We can't make out who it is.

Blackout.

SCENE TWO

Much later. Kate, Daniel, Carl, Ben and Laura are sitting round the dining-table drinking. There is half of a large chocolate cake left. Everyone is dressed much more smartly and has had lots to drink. Rebecca isn't there.

Laura I think I'll have a tiny slither more.

Ben Only a tiny one. We don't want you getting fat.

Kate That's nice.

Laura cuts herself a slice of cake with a large knife.

Laura Only twenty minutes to go. I'm so excited.

Rebecca comes back through the doorway leading to the library with Carl's wallet in her hand. She's been taking drugs in the bathroom. She sits down next to Carl and passes it to him under the table. No one else sees.

Daniel You should have some cake. You made it.

Rebecca I couldn't eat another thing. I'm stuffed.

Carl gets up and goes to the bathroom.

Laura You know what we must do. I do it every New Year's Eve. You go round and say what your low point and high point of the year was.

Daniel Oh no.

Kate I'm not really into things like that.

Ben Maybe we should just a pick a high point.

Daniel What if you can't even think of a high point?

Laura You've got to do both. That's how it works. You banish the bad and celebrate the good.

Rebecca I love all this. Then we can do favourite film of the year, favourite book, favourite exhibition . . .

Kate I'm just not keen on the whole lists thing, comparing everything.

Rebecca What does that mean?

Laura It's good. You put an end to the year. Evaluate it. Shall I go first?

Daniel If you must.

Laura So my high point was when I got to go to the *Glamour Magazine* Awards party at the Natural History Museum and I was wearing a –

Ben Did you go to that? I was at that.

Laura No.

Ben Yeah.

Laura No.

Ben Yeah.

Laura No.

Ben Yeah.

Laura No.

Daniel Somebody please stop them.

Kate I think he was there.

Ben I don't believe it.

Laura It was amazing.

Ben Amazing.

Laura Everyone was there. How come we didn't meet?

Ben Why didn't we meet?

Laura It just means we were meant to be together.

Kate No, it doesn't, because you didn't meet.

Ben It just means that then mustn't have been the right time.

Laura Yes.

Rebecca So that was your high point.

Laura Oh yeah, my low point . . .

She thinks.

Kate I'm guessing you might not have had one.

Laura I know. My lowest point was when my heel snapped at the *Glamour Magazine* Awards party at the Natural History Museum.

Kate That must have been awful.

Laura It was. Louboutin they were, too. Luckily it was on the way out.

Daniel I'm so relieved it wasn't on the way in.

Ben I'll go next. I think my high point of the year has to be meeting Laura.

Kate Of course.

Ben And my low point. I don't know, it's been a really great year. Maybe not meeting Laura at the *Glamour Magazine* Awards party at the Natural History Museum.

Rebecca Very good. Well done.

Laura Kate next.

Kate Let someone else do it.

Laura We're going round. It's your turn.

Rebecca Go on.

Kate Do I have to?

Daniel No.

Laura Yes.

Ben We've done it.

Kate I'd rather not.

Rebecca Come on, you're amongst friends.

Kate Maybe I'll do it the other way round.

Laura Oh yeah. Get the negative out of the way and end on a positive.

Pause.

Kate I think the lowest point for me was when Matthew told me he was leaving me. In an email. Or maybe it was when I had my second miscarriage? Or it could have been when my mother died? There's so many to choose from.

Pause.

Laura And what's your high point?

Daniel Maybe we shouldn't play this.

Rebecca And it was just getting interesting.

Ben Let's put some music on. Have a dance. I've got it all set up.

Ben goes to his iPhone which is sitting in its dock with speakers and sub-woofer attached and all laid out. He looks through the music.
Kate opens a bottle of wine slightly away from everyone else across the room. Carl comes out of the bathroom and goes over to Ben.

Kate Do we want music on?

Laura *and* **Rebecca** Yeah.

Ben scrolls through his music. Carl looks at the iPhone as he does so.

Ben Let me see.

Carl I can't believe I haven't got one yet.

Ben It's amazing. It makes me so happy. I've got my whole life on this. My diary, address book, maps, everything. I was the third person in London to have one, of the original ones. Camped out the night before. This is the latest version. I really don't know what I did before this. Look, look.

He opens an application and shows Carl. We can't see what it is. Ben wobbles the screen up and down. Carl laughs.

Carl That's brilliant.

Ben And look at this new thing it does.

Rebecca Where's the music?

Ben Okay. What shall we have? Old school or . . .

Ben puts his iPhone back in the dock.

Rebecca Something funky.

Kate tops up her empty wine glass.

Carl You alright?

Kate Yeah.

Ben Remember this?

'You Got the Love' by The Source, featuring Candi Staton, plays. Nods of recognition between Kate, Daniel, Carl and Ben.

Kate Oh God.

Laura screams and starts dancing about with Rebecca and Ben.

Rebecca I love this one. They played this at the Big Chill. (*To Kate.*) Come on, a good dance will cheer you up.

Kate In a minute.

Daniel (*quiet to Kate*) Couples on the loose. They've got a babysitter, their one chance to go mad and nothing's going to get in their way.

Rebecca continues to dance as she talks.

Rebecca (*to Kate*) Have you been to the Big Chill?

Kate No, no.

Rebecca Oh it's brilliant. It's a real grown-up festival. All thirty- and forty-somethings. Not grungey at all and everyone takes their kids.

Kate (*to Daniel*) Sounds great.

Daniel (*to Kate*) I went a few years ago, didn't I. It was hideous. Women in their forties, off their face on MDMA, gurning away with their kids on their shoulders. Dragging this poor child round an open-air nightclub.

Kate You can't leave me. You have to stay with me, keep me sane.

Daniel Don't worry, I'm going to be superglued to your side all night.

> *The music reaches a crescendo, as does Rebecca and Laura's dancing.*
> *The music blows and all the lights go off. It's pitch black. No light at all.*
> *Laura lets out a scream.*

Ben Oh shit.

Kate Thank fuck for that.

Carl What's happened there?

Laura I don't like it.

Ben It's alright, baby.

Daniel They've cut the power.

Kate Who's cut the power?

Daniel Whoever's outside. That's what they always do first, cut the power.

Laura Please don't say that.

Ben Pack it in, Daniel.

Kate It's blown a fuse. (*To Ben.*) That'll be your sound system.

Ben It's nothing to do with me. It better not be damaged.

Carl flicks the light switch on and off.

Carl Yeah, it's gone. Did anyone bring a torch?

Daniel What d'you reckon?

Kate There's some candles in the kitchen. And the fusebox.

Laura lets out a short scream.

Ben What is it?

Laura What's that? I think it's the sofa.

Ben Just keep still. I'll find you.

Carl Who's that?

Kate It's me.

Ben I'm here now, baby.

Rebecca Will you take your hand off my arse please, Ben?

Ben Sorry.

Laura knocks into a table and sends what sounds like some books crashing to the floor.

Kate Careful.

Laura I don't like it.

Ben Keep still. I'll come to you.

Laura Is that you, baby?

Ben Could be.

Laura giggles. They start snogging loudly.

Kate Can you two keep your hands off each other for a minute?

Laura There's someone or something outside.

Kate Don't start that again.

Laura There is . . . Listen.

Pause. They all listen. There's no sound.

Rebecca There's no one there.

Movement can be heard outside. A glimmer of moonlight lights the room.

Laura There's something out there.

Carl Where's the Valium?

Ben It'll be Lou and Mini.

Kate It's not them. They're not coming.

Ben Oh, aren't they?

Carl Why not?

Kate Shush.

There's movement outside the window.

Carl Look, there's someone there.

Rebecca Go out and see.

Carl No.

Kate It'll just be the trees.

Daniel It could be someone from the local village.

Kate Doing what? It's not like they're going to be passing.

Ben It could be an animal.

Kate Oh well, that's alright then. It's just a big animal walking around outside.

Laura What sort of animal?

Carl Like a wild dog?

Daniel Yeah, like the Hound of the Baskervilles.

Kate It could be a fox, or a badger.

Laura A baby badger! Or a cute little beaver or otter.

Rebecca Will someone sort out the lights?

Kate I'll have a look in the kitchen. Will one of you come with me?

Carl Okay. Are you frightened?

Kate Are you coming or not?

Kate and Carl go off to the kitchen.

Daniel I'm going to have a look.

Laura Don't.

Daniel This is ridiculous. There's nothing to be scared of.

Laura But if you open the door it could come right in. At least we're safe with the door locked.

Daniel You've been watching too many horror films.

Laura And the one thing you learn from horror films is don't go towards the noise.

The power and lights come back on.
Daniel moves to open the door.

Yay! Please don't open it.

Ben Let's just forget all about it.

Kate and Carl come through with lit candles.

Kate Some dodgy wiring through there. We'll light these as back-up.

They light more and place them around the room.
Laura takes in the room.

Laura Ah look at it now, it's all magical.

Ben looks over at where his iPhone was. It's not there.

Ben Where's my . . .

He finds it on the floor.

What the . . . (*To Laura.*) Did you knock it off?

Laura I don't know. Did I?

Ben picks it up from the floor very delicately. He looks at it in his hand. He can't speak.

Kate What is it?

Ben I don't believe it. The . . . It's . . . It's got a huge crack across the screen . . . like someone's stood on it.

Laura Was that me?

He tries to turn it on.

Ben I told you to stand still. What were you doing, still walking around when I told you to not to move?

Laura I was scared.

Ben It's not working. It won't come on. It's completely fuckin' broken.

Laura It was an accident.

Ben (*to Laura*) I've got everything on here, everything.

Kate Hey, she didn't do it on purpose.

Laura I'm sorry.

Daniel You've got it all backed up, haven't you?

Ben Some of it, but that's not the point.

Carl Let me have a look. They're quite resilient, these little buggers. (*He looks at it.*) Oh dear.

He hands it back to Ben.

Ben It's fucked, it's completely fucked.

Ben looks at his broken iPhone. He's almost in tears. Pause.

Rebecca What do we do now?

Ben Might as well put these speakers away, won't be needing them.

He abruptly puts his speakers away.

Laura Oh my God, there's something outside again. I just saw it go past the window.

Ben There's no one outside, there wasn't before and there isn't now. Will you stop going on about it!

Pause.
There's a loud knock on the knocker at the door.

Kate You are joking.

Laura Oh my God, oh my God . . .

She starts breathing heavily again.

Rebecca Are we expecting someone?

Daniel Do you think it's some escaped psycho? A serial killer?

Laura lets out a yelp.

Carl Daniel!

Laura I told you. I knew it, I knew it.

Kate Yeah, and I think he knocks on the door before he slaughters everyone.

Carl Where's that friggin' Valium?

Rebecca Who's going to answer it?

Nobody moves.

Laura It might just go away.

Kate (*to Carl*) Go on.

Carl I'm not getting it. You get it.

Kate looks to Ben.

Ben Don't look at me.

Daniel Fuck it. I'll get it. What's the worst it could be? Don't answer that.

Daniel goes up to the door to answer it. He slowly opens the door ajar. He doesn't open the door fully, and we can't see who's there.

Hello?

The person on the other side, Adam, answers in hushed tones. He has a slight accent from the local area. We can't fully hear what's being said.

Adam (*off*) Hi, it's Adam.

Daniel goes into the opening of the door, blocking the view.

Daniel (*off*) Oh shit. What are you doing here?

Adam (*off*) I've come to see you.

Kate Who is it?

Rebecca Does he know them?

Daniel (*off*) But . . .

Adam (*off*) Can I come in?

Daniel (*off*) Not really.

Adam (*off*) But . . .

Daniel (*off*) You shouldn't have come here.

Carl Who is it?

Daniel (*off*) This is not the time. You'll have to go.

Rebecca goes up and opens the door fully to reveal a twenty-two-year-old lad called Adam standing outside. He's wearing a black hooded top with the hood up.

Rebecca Hello.

Adam Hello.

Rebecca Do you two know each other?

Daniel No.

Adam (*at the same time*) Yes.

Rebecca Which one is it?

Daniel We do know each other.

Rebecca Well, come on in then.

Adam (*to Daniel*) Are you sure?

Daniel Sure. Come on in. Yeah.

Adam comes in. He takes down his hood. Daniel closes the door behind him.

So, here we are . . . Do you want a drink?

Adam Yeah, okay.

Daniel What d'you want? There's . . .

Daniel moves to lead Adam over to the drinks.

Kate Aren't you going to introduce us?

Daniel Oh right. This is . . . Adam.

Adam smiles. They wait to be introduced by Daniel. It doesn't happen.

67

Kate Hiya, I'm Kate.

Daniel Oh, sorry. And this is Carl.

Carl Alright.

Daniel Ben and Laura.

Ben Hi.

Laura gives a little wave.

Daniel Rebecca.

Rebecca Hello, Adam.

Adam Alright.

Daniel (*to Adam*) What d'you want?

Adam Don't mind. A beer?

The others are all waiting for an explanation.

Kate Did you know Adam was coming?

Daniel Not really.

Rebecca Were you just passing? On a horse perhaps?

Daniel Adam lives in the village here.

Kate Right.

Daniel It's the strangest thing. Adam . . . and me . . . work together . . . And I bumped into him in the village earlier. How weird is that?

Rebecca It's almost unbelievable.

Kate You're an architect?

Daniel Yeah.

Rebecca And you work in London, but you live out here.

Daniel He's sort of freelance.

Rebecca Can Adam speak?

Daniel tries to laugh it off.

Daniel Of course. (*To Adam.*) Beer's in the fridge.

Daniel goes off to the kitchen with Adam.

Carl What's that all about?

Rebecca (*to Kate*) Did he tell you he was expecting a visitor?

Kate No.

Rebecca You know what gays are like, they're like magnets. They always seek each other out. That boy probably went round knocking on doors till he found one. I bet you they've never met before. (*She sees that her glass is empty.*) I need more wine.

Rebecca heads off to the kitchen.
  Kate and Carl go back to lighting more candles round the room.
  Laura joins a quiet Ben, who's on the sofa looking at his broken iPhone.

Laura Baby, you know . . .

Ben In a minute.

Ben gets up and goes over to Carl, who's just out of earshot of Laura.

You got any . . .

Carl Yeah, yeah.

Carl passes Ben the wallet with the drugs in.

Ben Cheers.

Ben hurries off to the bathroom.
  Laura looks at her watch.

Laura Oh my God. Look at the time. Five minutes. Sparklers, where are the sparklers?

Laura goes off towards the bedrooms. She lets out a frightened squeak at the dark doorway but bravely goes through.
  Kate and Carl are left alone.

Carl We need to talk?

Kate Do we?

Carl Yeah.

Kate I don't want to know.

Carl Oh come on . . .

Kate What have you taken? Are you off your face?

Carl No.

Kate Have you been doing drugs with her?

Carl No.

Carl gurns slightly.

Kate Look at you.

Carl It's New Year's Eve, it's a party. D'you want some?

Kate No. I can't believe she's doing drugs. What's got into her?

Carl Anyway . . .

Kate I can't talk to you while you're like this.

Carl This would have been you not all that long ago.

Rebecca comes in from the kitchen with a fresh bottle of red wine and a full glass.
  Kate and Carl break apart.

Rebecca I didn't realise the time. Not long now.

Rebecca walks over to Carl. She puts her arm round him. Kate tries to look busy.

I feel like we've hardly spoken all night. (*Quietly.*) Where is it?

Carl Ben's got it, in the bathroom.

Rebecca What did you give it to him for?

Carl 'Cause I wanted to.

Rebecca I don't want him to know we've got it, he'll be after it all night.

Carl He won't and there's loads. Anyway, I paid for it.

Rebecca With my money.

Carl What's that supposed to mean?

Rebecca Will you go and get it off him for me?

Carl If you want it, you go and get it.

Rebecca goes off on a little tour of the room, looking out of the window as she does, all to disguise her ultimate destination, the doorway leading to the bathroom. She casually disappears through it.

Kate That was subtle.

Carl comes back over to Kate.

Carl You know how I feel.

Kate Go away, Carl.

Carl Kate.

Kate I thought this was going to be our chance to . . .

Carl It's all going to be alright . . .

Kate I thought we'd be together at midnight. Start the New Year . . .

Carl We still can . . .

Daniel and Adam come out of the kitchen with their drinks. Daniel joins Kate.

Daniel (*to Adam*) Two secs . . .

Adam goes over to the table and picks at some food. Carl goes over to the corridor leading down to the bathroom. He looks down the corridor to Rebecca.

Carl (*to Rebecca down the corridor*) Knock on the door, he's in there . . . For fuck's sake.

He goes down the hall.

Daniel You alright with this?

Kate Who is he?

Daniel He's a friend from work. He doesn't actually live down here, he's visiting his parents.

Kate Is that the revised version? Credit me with a bit of intelligence.

Daniel Don't you believe me?

Kate None of us believe you.

Daniel I met him on the internet.

Kate When? How? When you were making dinner?

Daniel About a month ago. We've been chatting since then. He's really sweet.

Kate What d'you know about him?

Daniel We both like the same sort of music, he's into graphic novels like me . . .

Kate Graphic novels? Since when?

Daniel I like them, I do. I read them all the time.

Kate I mean what sort of weirdo is he? Wandering round outside for hours.

Daniel How do you know that was him?

Kate Oh, have you got a selection of desperate gayboys hanging round outside?

Daniel It could have been anyone.

Kate That's reassuring. You know, we've come here as a group of friends and you thought you'd organise a shag?

Daniel I didn't ask him to come. I told him we were staying here and he just took it upon himself to turn up.

Kate Oh great, even weirder. But you were going to meet him anyway? Is that why you were umming and aahing about coming? You had to check if there'd be any fresh meat nearby?

Daniel It wasn't like that. I was just bored in work one day and thought I'd see what was going on round here. Graham says if I want to meet people off the internet, then that's okay. I don't have to be ashamed of it.

Kate Don't start using your new therapist to justify your actions.

Daniel He says it's a legitimate way for minorities to meet.

Kate Graham would think this is a good idea, would he?

Daniel And he's not just a shag. I really like him.

Kate You don't even know him. Does his mum and dad know he's here?

Daniel He's not that young.

Kate Just get rid of him.

Daniel What?

Kate He's not invited. I don't want to spend my New Year with some teenager I don't know.

Daniel What happened to 'I'm free and easy, anyone can come and go'?

Kate I've changed my mind.

Daniel I can't just tell him to go.

Kate I'll do it for you, if you want.

Daniel What's got into you?

Adam walks over, he appears behind them.

Let me show you the rest of the house.

*They both head off towards the bedrooms.
Carl comes back in.*

Carl She's doing my head in. Fuckin' pain in the arse.

Carl goes over to Kate. He comes close and tries to kiss her.

Kate No, Carl, no. We're just good, close friends, nothing more.

Carl We're more than that. The last couple of months you've been everything to me.

Kate I don't want to hear this.

Carl Why did we ever split up?

Kate You know why.

Carl But it was right, we were so good together.

Kate It's in the past . . .

Carl If it wasn't for the kids I would have left her like that. You know I . . .

Kate Carl, you're drunk, you're off your face.

Carl I want to be with you.

Kate Well, you can't have everything you want. You're with her.

Carl I know you feel the same.

Kate No, Carl . . .

Carl I'm going to leave her. I can't do this any more.

Kate You've said that before.

Carl I'm not going to go back to London with her.

Kate What?

Carl I can't go back home with her. If I do I'll never leave her.

Kate Carl.

Carl I'm going to do it, I have to.

Kate Are you serious?

*Carl looks into her eyes and kisses Kate passionately.
Kate reciprocates.*
  *They break apart just as Laura comes back with a
pack of sparklers. She hands Kate and Carl one each.*

Laura Sparklers. You've got to have sparklers. It's like a minute to go. Where is everyone? Where's Ben?

Carl goes off to the kitchen.
  *Ben comes back in from the bathroom. He heads
over to the bar to make himself a stiff drink. He's
looking intense.*

There you are, baby. Sparkler.

She holds out a sparkler. He doesn't take it.

Sparkler, baby.

75

Ben I don't want one.

Laura Please take one.

Kate (*snappy*) Have a sparkler, Ben. It's New Year's Eve.

Ben takes it and puts it down on the drinks table.

Laura Where's Daniel and his friend Adam?

Kate They better hadn't of gone to bed.

Laura They can't have. We haven't done midnight yet. Where's Rebecca?

Kate Powdering her nose, no doubt.

Carl comes in with a bottle of champagne in a bucket, glasses on a tray and a fruit juice for Laura.

Carl Let's open some more champagne for midnight.

Laura The bread and coal! What about the bread and coal?

Kate Forget it. (*To Carl.*) I hate New Year.

Carl Don't. This'll be a good one.

Carl pops the champagne cork and pours out glasses.
  Rebecca comes out of the toilet with a nosebleed.
She's not aware of it.

Rebecca Bring on the New Year.

Carl I think you need a tissue. Nosebleed.

She goes back down the corridor to the toilet.
  Ben sits down and looks at his broken iPhone longingly.
  Carl goes round giving everyone a glass of champagne.
  Laura looks at her watch.

Laura Ten seconds!

Kate Where the hell is Daniel?

Kate goes off through the doorway to the bedrooms to look.
  Laura starts counting down from ten, as she lights everyone's sparklers round the room.

Laura Ten . . . (*To Ben.*) Where's your sparkler? Nine . . .

She picks it back up and gives it to him.

Here it is. Eight . . .

Rebecca comes out of the toilet, blood gone.

Rebecca That's better.

Laura Seven . . . Quick.

Laura gives Rebecca a sparkler.

Six . . .

Kate comes back.

Kate His door's shut. I don't believe it.

Laura Five . . .

Carl (*to Laura*) Fruit juice for you.

He hands Laura the fruit juice.

Laura Thank you, lovely. Four . . .

Kate Is he shagging that boy?

Laura Three . . .

Rebecca joins Carl, putting her arms round him.

Rebecca I wish the kids were here.

Laura Two . . .

Laura goes over to Ben.

I'm so excited. One . . . Happy New Year, everyone!

Rebecca Happy New Year, darling.

Carl Happy New Year.

Rebecca kisses Carl and holds him tight.

Laura (*to Ben*) Happy New Year, baby.

Laura moves to kiss him. He gives her his cheek.

Kate (*quietly*) Happy New Year.

Kate stands in the middle of the room on her own with a sparkler in her hand.
  She starts to cry quietly.
  Blackout.

End of Act One.

Act Two

We can just see the back of what looks like a long blonde-haired woman in a floaty seventies dress drinking and smoking a cigarette at the open front door. It's pitch black outside. It should seem like we are at a different time, almost dreamlike. Candles light the room and the fire is lit in the fireplace.

Ben comes out from the doorway leading to the library in a red wig and short retro dress. He checks himself out in a mirror across the room.

Ben I think this is a bit tight. It doesn't show my figure off to its best.

The blonde woman turns and we see it's Carl in a blonde wig. Everyone has attacked the dressing-up box, some more than others. Some with just a funny hat. Through this scene their dressing-up clothes become more dishevelled, bits falling off, and they become less aware of them.

Carl Yeah, quite hippy. Makes your bum look too big.

Ben Hmm, yeah.

Carl And the blue really brought out your eyes.

Ben But this hair's good.

Carl The red's good, keep the red.

Ben goes back through the doorway. Kate comes in from outside. She's wearing just a few items of dressing-up clothes on top of her normal clothes.

79

Kate It's a beautiful night. So clear, you can see fireworks for miles.

Carl Where's she gone?

Kate Through some bushes to try and get a signal. I can't see her.

Carl Shall we lock the door?

Pause.

Kate I've never cried at midnight before. Never understood that whole thing. I remember when I was a kid at New Year's parties and at twelve o'clock my Auntie Maureen would always be crying. Every year. I used to think, 'What's wrong with her? We're at a party. What have you got to cry about?'

Carl I hate seeing you upset.

Kate It's going to be a good year.

Carl Your book's coming out.

Kate I'm still in with a chance to make things happen. My life could still be good. I reckon I've got a couple more years to turn it round . . . if it doesn't work out then . . .

Carl Then what?

Kate I'd just have to resign myself to the fact that my life didn't turn out the way I wanted it to. I wouldn't be able to hang round with successful people any more. It's a bit too much already, but I'm still hopeful. If it doesn't work out I'll have to surround myself with people even worse off to make me feel better.

Carl Is that why you like me? Because I'm such a fuck-up.

Kate No. Maybe.

Carl You're . . . We're going to be alright. We can be fuck-ups together.

Kate Can we?

Carl I tasted a bit of success. Worked loads when I was young. But when I lost my looks, to quote Rebecca, it all went downhill. You know I haven't worked since that last coffee commercial . . . that was four years ago. Something could turn up, get cast in some big series. But maybe I don't want it any more. Rebecca tries to set up meetings for me, but I don't want to know. She put me forward for one of her shows but I turned it down. I'd rather get it on my own merits, not as some backhander. The garden centre keeps me happy.

Kate You and your potted palms.

Carl I like it. It's really peaceful. Plant some plants, chat to the dotty customers, read a book. It's great. I finish at the end of the day and that's it. Rebecca's all worried about how it looks. She told some director who'd seen me that I was doing research for a Mike Leigh film.

Kate She didn't?

Carl Or she says I should run my own garden centre or become a TV gardener. I can't just be a bloke who works in a garden centre. You know, since Rebecca has had her success more people acknowledge me now. Directors and actors who I hardly know, or who'd decided I had the whiff of failure about me, can't get enough of me now. After this book, they'll be all over you.

Kate I don't know about that.

Carl Success is overrated anyway. Look at Rebecca. She's miserable most of the time. She can never relax, always has to be doing something. Always has to be achieving.

Kate I suppose if you were content you wouldn't keep striving for something else.

Carl And she treats people like shit. If they can't do anything for her, she doesn't want to know. She's got no loyalty whatsoever. It's all about her and her ascent. And you should see her work friends, these other media fools. They've all got something wrong with them. Some huge personality flaw. You get them together, it's like day release from the asylum. All twitching and itching and unable to make eye contact. And they're all really short. Do I sound bitter?

Kate I sometimes think that success comes from a bad place. I've written some of my best work driven by jealousy and envy. When I wrote that short story a few years back that was published in the anthology.

Carl 'The Butterfly'.

Kate Yeah, 'The Butterfly'.

Carl I loved that.

Kate Ah. I had the names of other writers I know, who I think are shit but do well, written across my wall. If I was flagging I'd look up and see 'Philip Andrews' and that would fire me on.

   Pause.

Kate Maybe it could be alright to fail. There's no book.

Carl You what?

Kate It's not coming out next year. It's been turned down by every publisher in town.

Carl It'll get picked up.

Kate I don't think it will. Maybe it's a pile of crap. I've written a bad book.

Carl You won't have.

Kate But why can't it be alright to do something shit, to fail, for everything not to be perfect. Or to be even allowed to say that and not be thought of as a lesser human being. I haven't even told anyone else. I'm too ashamed. Failure's the worst thing. We're all doing it, all lying to each other.

Carl 'I've got a few things in the pipeline . . .' My wonderful acting career.

Kate Everyone thinks Daniel's designing London's tallest building but he's in charge of the door handles and the disabled toilets. He doesn't even know I know that. And I don't know what's going on with Ben.

Carl Gi's a kiss.

He pulls Kate towards him.

Kate Rebecca might see.

Carl The sooner she knows the better.

Kate Yeah, but . . .

Kate tries to move away.

Carl She knows it's on the cards. You've seen what we're like together. It's doomed. It's okay when we're with the kids, but . . . even that's chaos. Christmas was fine. We can't just stay together for them, that's the cowardly thing to do.

Kate I never thought I'd be back here with you. But it feels right.

She kisses him.

This is how I imagined it'd be. We going to be alright?

Carl Yeah.

Kate Yeah?

Carl You've got nothing to worry about.

Ben comes back in with a blue dress on.

Now you're talking.

Ben I think I make a really good woman.

Carl You've got a great rack.

Ben I'm very proud of my tits. Got a lovely pair.

Laura comes in from the bedrooms with a brightly coloured dress and a fancy hat on.

Laura I really can't decide what to put on. What d'you think?

Carl I think the dress is too much.

Laura This is my own dress.

Carl It's not?

Laura nods.
Carl and Ben burst out laughing and find it hard to stop.

Kate Ignore them. I think the hat looks lovely.

Laura Maybe I'll . . . Can we close the door, please?

Kate Rebecca's still out there.

Laura *(to Carl)* Shouldn't you be out there with her?

Carl and Ben continue to laugh.

Carl I'm grateful for the peace.

Ben Let's have a pool tournament in these.

Carl Oh yeah.

Ben Let me take some pictures on my . . . *(He moves to get his iPhone.)* Oh no . . .

Carl Doesn't matter. Come on, come on.

Carl grabs Ben and they head off towards the doorway to the library.

Ben Have you got the . . .

Carl Rebecca's got it. When she comes back I'll . . .

Laura Can I come and play?

Ben doesn't answer.

Carl Of course you can.

Laura I'll just try something else on first.

Carl and Ben disappear off through the doorway leading to the library. Laura looks at herself in the mirror.
Kate's at the door.

Kate She has been gone quite a long time now.

Kate steps out onto the step and looks out.
Laura heads towards the dressing-up cupboard, passing the drinks table. There's various open bottles and drinks there. She pauses for a second, sees that Kate is outside and quickly pours herself a large glass of wine. She takes a sip, then a big gulp and quickly tops up the glass. She heads across the room with the glass.

I'm sure she's fine.

Kate closes the door. Laura passes Kate and smiles. She half hides the wine from Kate. Laura goes off through the doorway leading to the library.
Kate is left alone. Not sure what to do with herself. She picks up her drink and takes in the room.
Adam comes through. He heads over to the drinks table and starts to make two fresh drinks.

Adam Just getting a top up.

85

Kate I didn't think we'd be seeing you again tonight.

Pause. Adam makes the drinks.

Adam Did anyone believe that I was really his mate from work?

Kate What d'you think?

Adam I'm used to pretending to be someone else. That's how it works, especially round here with all the small villages and holiday homes. I've been everyone. Old friends, a brother, even a trainee priest. It's the older guys that do all that stuff. Anyone my age just introduces me as a shag they've met on the internet.

Kate The joys of youth.

Adam I love the internet. You can find anything you want on there. See whatever you want. It shows you the world. Is David okay?

Kate D'you mean Daniel?

Adam Yeah, yeah.

Kate I think so.

Adam He seemed a bit weird.

Kate Maybe he's had too much to drink.

Adam Can I have some cake?

Kate Sure.

Adam picks up the large sharp knife that was used to cut the cake. He holds it in his hand and gesticulates with it as he talks. Kate is slightly unnerved by this.

Adam You never know what you're gonna get when you meet blokes off the internet. They hardly ever look like their photo. But he's just . . . We've been chatting for a few weeks and he seemed really keen. Always online, even during the day when he's at work. Replies straight away. I liked that. And it all started getting a bit sexy, dirty, you know. Him saying what we were gonna do.

Kate Listen, I . . .

Adam It's alright. We'd got into that sexy texting and it was good, really good. That's why I'm here. I thought I'm not going to miss out on this one. But when it came down to it he just wanted to . . . talk. And then just when I thought we were getting somewhere he said he just wanted someone to hold him. So we just ended up hugging. I've come all this way for a shag, that's the last thing I want. I kept on trying to get down to it but nothing was happening.

Adam cuts a slice of cake and eats it in his hands. He puts the knife back on the plate with the cake.

Kate Well, the night is young. You've still got plenty of time to 'get down to it'.

Adam You know what. I think I'm gonna get off. This is not for me.

Kate But . . .

Adam I don't know if I can wait around, to see what happens. I'm gonna go. There's some other bloke I've been chatting to at a Landmark Trust place across the way. If I'm lucky . . .

Adam stuffs the last of the cake in his mouth and goes off into the kitchen. Kate gets up and goes over to the doorway leading to the bedrooms to see if Daniel is about. Adam comes back on, zipping up his jacket.

Kate Does Daniel know you're going?

Adam Naah.

Kate Let me just go and get him. Let him say goodbye.

Adam Naah, it's too messy. He could tell it wasn't working. I think he knows I'd probably go.

Adam opens the door fully to leave. Laura comes out, she's got more dressing-up clothes on and a wine glass in hand.

Laura You're not going already? We've hardly got to know each other. You don't want to go outside on your own. Aren't you scared of it out there?

Adam I'm fine. See ya.

She gives him a big hug and kiss. Adam heads out, closing the door behind him.

Laura Bye. He was lovely. I love the gays. He was, wasn't he?

Kate Yeah, well spotted.

Laura I hope he's going to be okay. With whatever's out there.

Kate It was him. He was out there.

Laura Was it though? I don't think it was.

She tops up her drink.

Kate You're drinking. Sorry, I thought you didn't drink. Didn't like the taste.

Laura I just felt like one and this one tastes nice.

Pause.

Do you think I look fat?

Kate God no, there's nothing of you.

Laura Are you happy?

Kate Well . . . Who's happy?

Laura Are you happy being single?

Kate I wouldn't consider myself as single. I'm just me.

Laura That's why you're single. You don't want it enough.

Kate If you say so.

Laura How old are you? Thirty-nine?

Kate I'm thirty-six.

Laura You haven't got much time.

Kate What for?

Laura Babies. Children. That clock is ticking. From thirty-five your chances of getting pregnant just plummet.

Kate I know.

Laura Do you want kids?

Kate Well . . . If it happens . . .

Laura You've got to make it happen.

Kate It does involve someone else.

Laura Not necessarily. If I hadn't met Ben I would have well had my eggs frozen by the time I got to your age. You've only got this one chance to have children and if you don't take it, that'll be it for ever.

Kate Anyway . . .

Laura Do you ever pray?

Kate No. I did go to church the other day . . .

Laura And how was it?

Kate I quite liked it.

Laura You see. If I want something, I get down on my knees and pray. If you ask for it, it'll come to you. I prayed for a boyfriend and that night I met Ben. A friend of a friend lost his job, was broke, was about to be made homeless. He prayed to the HP, higher power, and the next day he won the lottery.

Kate Is that right?

Laura Apparently. Do you believe in God?

Kate No. I like the idea but just can't get my head round it. My mum believed in God, even when she was dying. She still had faith, a belief in something bigger. It gave her strength, I'd like that. Where is everyone?

Laura You don't have to believe in God, as God. You know, a big man in the clouds with a white beard. You just have to believe in something outside of yourself. (*She looks around for something.*) So this glass of wine, no, not that. My shoe could be God and I'd pray to that. I quite like that, praying to a big Balenciaga shoe. Aren't they beautiful. I'm not going to tell you how much they cost.

Kate Right.

Carl puts his head round the doorway to the library.

Carl Any sign of Rebecca?

Kate No.

Carl Give us a shout when she's back.

Kate Hang on . . .

But he's already gone.

Laura It's like the law of attraction, isn't it? Everything you bring into your life you ask for. Even when you don't think you're praying you are, you're asking for it . . .

Kate You know what . . .

Laura Most of the time we focus on what we don't want rather than what we want. So we say, 'I don't want to be fat,' and, 'I don't want to have frizzy hair,' and God, the universe, the Balenciaga shoe, just hears the 'fat' and 'frizzy hair' bits and gives them to you. Everything that happens to us we've made happen.

Kate I don't believe that.

Laura That's what everyone says at first. But you've got to take responsibility for your actions. Whatever happens to you is your fault.

Kate So my mum attracted the cancer into her? She asked for it? Wanted it?

Laura Er, I suppose so, on some level she must have . . .

Daniel comes through from the bedrooms.

Kate And people who are raped and murdered, they ask for it, do they?

Laura I'm not sure. That doesn't sound right.

Daniel How shall we start the New Year? Let's talk about rape and murder? (*To Kate.*) And what are you wearing?

Kate Someone found the dressing-up box.

Laura looks at her outfit.

Laura This isn't working.

Laura heads off through the doorway leading to the library with her wine glass, picking up a half-opened bottle of wine on the way.

Kate Oh God.

Daniel You're not still pissed off with me, are you?

Kate It's that lunatic. But listen –

Daniel Before you say anything. I'm sorry, he came. I really didn't plan it. Okay, I was probably going to sneak off and meet him at some point but I wouldn't invite someone round like that.

Kate It's okay . . .

Daniel (*whispering*) But I really like him. You know what I'm like, falling in love at the drop of a hat. Anyone who's half nice to me, I'm smitten. And I'm trying not to get carried away and remember what Graham's always telling me but . . . I think he's really special. There was a connection there straight away. We've just chatted and he really listened.

Kate Daniel . . .

Daniel He's really interested in me as a person. He's not just here to get his end away. I know he's young, a bit too young, but age doesn't matter. I can't remember the last time I've had a really good conversation with someone I've met on the . . . And I know everyone thinks it's sleazy but I think you can find love on there. Look at Steven and Mark, they've been together for . . . Where is he? Is he in the . . . (*He points towards the kitchen.*)

Kate He's gone.

Daniel Where?

Kate He's gone, left. He said goodbye.

Daniel What did you say to him? Did you tell him to go?

Kate I didn't say anything.

Daniel How long ago?

Kate Just now.

Daniel opens the door and looks out.

Daniel But . . .

Pause.

What did he say?

Kate Nothing really.

Daniel You can tell me.

Kate We hardly spoke. He just came through and then he was gone. He said he'd call you.

Daniel Did he?

Kate Yeah, yeah.

Daniel You never know if it's going to work out. What they'll be like. If they'll like you. And you've got this whole idea of them, whole fantasy, but you've never actually met. You start second-guessing them. Saying stuff you think they'll want to hear so they'll like you. (*He shuts the door.*) Little shit. We should check we haven't been robbed. I'm serious, that's probably why he was here. Which rooms did he go in? My jacket, he's stolen my fuckin' jacket. It was on the back of that chair.

Kate I hung it up in the kitchen.

Daniel Oh, okay. We should check he has really gone. Little freak, hanging round outside all night. He could still be out there. Oh well. Happy fuckin' New Year. Another shit year over. Another one begins. What, half an hour we've had, and already I feel like . . . Mojito?

Daniel starts making drinks.

Kate I'm alright. I'm going to call it a night.

Daniel It's only early.

Kate I want a fresh start in the morning.

Daniel Where's the axis of evil?

Kate Out looking for someone fresh to sacrifice.

Laura comes back in. She's changed into a long flowing seventies dress with lots of accessories.

Laura What d'you reckon to this?

Kate (*to Daniel*) As I said –

Daniel You can't leave me.

Rebecca appears at the window. Laura screams.

Laura Oh my God! (*Then calms.*) It's Rebecca.

Kate opens the door.
Rebecca come in from outside. She's also in some dressing-up clothes with a strange ram's-head hat on her head. She's got very muddy shoes on and is in floods of tears.

Kate What's wrong?

Laura What's happened to you? Have you been attacked by something outside?

Carl comes through with Ben.

Carl (*to Rebecca*) There you are.

Ben (*whispered*) Get the stuff.

Rebecca Oh Carl.

She runs into his arms crying.

Carl What is it?

Laura I told her she shouldn't go outside. We think she's been attacked.

Rebecca (*still in tears*) I just phoned home.

Daniel You got a signal? Where?

Daniel gets his phone out and looks at it.

Rebecca Through the bushes and up some hillock.

Carl What's wrong?

Kate Is everything alright?

Rebecca Clemmie was awake. My mum put her on the phone. She said, 'I want snuggles off Mummy.' I really miss them.

Kate Oh God.

Daniel Maybe it is time for bed.

Carl Is that it?

Rebecca She's been asking my mum if I was dead, if I was ever coming back.

Carl That witch of a mother probably put the idea in her head.

Rebecca She's obsessed by death these days. What am I doing here? I should be with my children. I think we should go back.

She moves to get her stuff.

Carl Now? We're not going anywhere. I'm drunk, you're drunk. Let's get you another drink.

Daniel Mojitos?

Carl Two of your best, barman.

Ben And me. You make the most amazing mojitos.

Ben sits down on the sofa. He's trying to stay jolly but a darkness is seeping through.
Kate tidies up a bit.
Laura checks out her outfit in the mirror.
Daniel goes off to the kitchen to get mojito ingredients.
Carl takes Rebecca off to one corner. He thinks he's being subtle.

Carl (*whispering*) Give us the –

Rebecca I'm going first.

Carl I think you need to lay off it.

Rebecca Don't tell me what to do . . .

Carl Look at the state of you.

Rebecca Fuck off.

Carl Fuck you.

Rebecca Have the fuckin' stuff.

She shoves the wallet into Carl's hands.

I've had enough of this shit party. I told you we should
have gone to Simon Newton's.

Carl You can't stand him.

Rebecca Yeah, but there would have been some really
important people there.

*Rebecca sits at the table and looks at photos of her
children on her phone. Daniel comes back with mojito
ingredients and gets to work making them. Carl gives
him a hand.*
Kate's not sure what to do with herself.
*Laura joins Ben on the other sofa. They talk out of
earshot of everyone else.*

Laura I've missed you.

He doesn't answer. Pause.

You alright, baby?

Ben Yeah.

Pause.

Laura You're not still angry with me are you about your
gadget thingy?

Ben No. No.

Laura You'd tell me if you were.

Ben I'm fine. I didn't realise you were so clumsy.

Laura It was dark. I'm not normally so . . .

Ben It's good to know.

Pause.

I wonder if anyone's trying to contact me.

Laura D'you think . . . ?

Ben Don't know, do I?

Laura I could try and call anyone who you thought might be trying to call you, to see if they were and . . .

Ben Don't worry yourself. Just hope there's no important work things in the next few days.

Pause.

Shame we've got no music now . . .

Laura Why don't we play some games? You told me you love playing games. What's that one where you put all the names in a hat?

Ben Names in the hat?

Laura That's the one. Let's play that.

Ben Maybe later.

Laura What do you think of my outfit?

Ben Hmm, yeah.

Pause.

Laura I think I'll change into something else.

*Laura heads out through the doorway to the library
and surreptitiously grabs a bottle of whisky on the
way out.*
Kate looks over and sees Ben looking intense.

Kate (*to Carl nearby*) Is Ben . . . ?

Carl Don't worry.

Rebecca (*to Daniel*) Did I just see your 'best mate from
work' leaving before?

Daniel He was only calling by . . .

Rebecca God, you were quick. Was it literally 'get 'em
off, quick-one-two, then see you later, alligator'?

Daniel We didn't have sex, okay.

Rebecca Couldn't you get it up?

Daniel It's not all about sex, you know.

Rebecca What did he come round for? Had he heard
about your mojitos?

Carl Ignore her. That's what I do.

Kate joins Ben on the sofa. Ben turns on the smiles.

Kate Hiya. You . . . ?

Ben Having a brilliant time. It's so great you got us all
together. We should do more things like this.

Kate Maybe . . .

Ben I love this house. Can you imagine if this was yours?
If you lived here.

Kate I'm not sure . . .

Ben Or something like this in London. I love New Year.
Always have a great one. Last year it was Sydney. We had
a boat on the harbour, in front of the bridge, prime

position. All the fireworks. Amazing. Year before it was skiing in . . .

Kate Is Laura . . .

Ben She's loving it. In the party spirit. No stopping her.

Kate And you and her . . .

Ben Great, great. (*To Daniel.*) How are those mojitos coming on?

Daniel Getting there.

Kate You just looked a bit quiet. It's not like you. I was . . .

Ben I'm great.

Kate As long as you're . . .

Ben It's all great. You enjoy yourself.

He gets up to join Daniel and Carl making the cocktails.

I think you need a hand.

Kate moves to get up, but Rebecca joins her on the sofa. She's tearful from looking at the photos on her phone.

Rebecca Look at them. (*She shows Kate photos on her phone.*) That's Clementine. That's me and Clementine. That's me, Archie and Clementine. That's . . .

Kate You know what, I think I'm going to retire . . .

She gets up.

Rebecca No, I'm not letting you go. I haven't had a proper conversation with you all night.

Kate We'll have plenty of time to catch up tomorrow.

Rebecca Sit.

Kate reluctantly sits down.

I want to hear all about you. You've had such a tough year, but you've done really well. It's so great you've finished your book. Put all that Matthew business behind you.

Kate Life carries on.

Rebecca I bumped into him the other week with her. If it's any consolation she looked really rough. And she was massive . . .

Kate looks at her blankly.

Kate She's having a baby?

Carl (*to Rebecca*) You're on fire tonight.

Rebecca Didn't you know?

Carl Clearly not.

Rebecca I'm so sorry. She's due in a couple of weeks.

Kate It must have been someone else. She can't be.

Rebecca I'm sure . . . He introduced her as . . .

Kate But we didn't split up till July. If she's due soon, that would mean he was already . . .

Rebecca Oh God, I'm sorry.

Kate The . . .

Pause.

It shouldn't come as a surprise . . . So how long had he been . . .

Rebecca Well, he'll have an eye-opener once the baby comes along. That'll test them. He's having a mid-life crisis. She's just out of nappies herself, it won't work. The hardest thing you'll ever do. Ours are going through a right thing at the moment. Especially Clemmie. She's turned against her best friend, Scarlett, at nursery. Been so nasty to her. Saying she's ugly and her games are boring. She's got a point, her games are dull and she's not the prettiest, but it is awful.

Daniel Somewhere along the way she thinks that it's okay to say those sort of things.

Rebecca She hasn't got it from me.

Carl I couldn't think where she got her nastiness from.

Daniel Mojitos, everyone.

Daniel passes round mojitos to everyone.

Carl (*to Ben with a wink*) Pool?

Ben Yeah, yeah, yeah.

They both go off to the bathroom together.
Daniel offers a mojito to Kate.

Kate I didn't . . .

Daniel Take it.

Kate takes the drink.

Rebecca Needs more mint.

Rebecca goes off to the kitchen.

Kate Can we please stop talking about children all the time?

Daniel I know.

Kate I spend my whole life having other people's kids forced down my throat. I thought this'd be a break from all that. All my female friends apart from Lou and Mini, who I now also hate, have got kids, and that's all they go on about.

Daniel Maybe you should be done with it and get some yourself.

Kate Maybe it'll happen, maybe it won't. I've made peace with it. There's other things in life that can bring you joy, there has to be. I'm not going to be one of those crazy women in their late thirties who becomes obsessed with having a baby.

Daniel I've thought about it myself.

Kate No?

Daniel Even I feel the pressure. Do I join the gang, join the rest of society, or feel left out? In work, if we have to stay late we go round and all the mothers and even the fathers say they can't and then it gets to me and it's always, 'Daniel can stay.' Like my life is less valid. Whatever I was doing doesn't matter. 'You're just seeing your friends or going the pictures.'

Kate That's their problem, not yours.

Daniel But is my life going to be exactly the same in ten, twenty years' time? Will I just have more stuff? Go on more expensive holidays? Work harder?

Kate It can be whatever you make it.

Daniel We could . . .

Kate Don't be stupid.

Daniel Why don't we think about it?

Kate No.

Daniel I think we'd make great parents. They'd be really attractive.

Kate looks at him. It's a clear no.

Okay. Just because I can go off and make a baby doesn't mean I have to. And Graham said the answer in dealing with envy isn't to go and get what everyone else has got.

Kate Get a dog.

Rebecca comes back on, laughing to herself.

Rebecca I've remembered another thing Clemmie said . . .

Kate tuts.

What was that?

Kate Nothing.

Rebecca No, you just tutted when I mentioned my daughter.

Kate I don't know, did I? It doesn't matter.

Rebecca It does matter. How rude. Am I annoying you?

Kate No, no, let's just forget it.

Rebecca I've seen the little looks between the two of you.

Daniel What?

Rebecca The eye-rolling. You think I'm boring because I've got kids.

Daniel No, we don't.

Rebecca I'm not an idiot. I know what's going on here.

Daniel There's nothing going on.

Kate Well, maybe . . . You did say when you got here you weren't going to be one of those people who keeps talking about their kids, and then . . .

Laura comes back on, she's gone to town on the dressing-up box and thrown loads of different accessories on. She's got a bottle in her hand.

Laura What d'you think?

Daniel Great. Lovely.

Pause.

Rebecca Why wouldn't you want to hear about someone's children?

Kate Let's just forget about it, shall we?

Daniel Yeah.

Rebecca They're the most precious things in the world.

Kate I'm sure they are, but they're not here, so . . .

Laura What's happening?

Rebecca Why shouldn't I talk about them? I'm so proud of them, they're the most important things in my life.

Kate We know.

Daniel I think this is getting . . .

Rebecca What else is as important as your children? Why would you be so nasty about them?

Kate I'm not being nasty. I just think there's other topics of conversation.

Rebecca Like what? What should we be talking about?

Kate Anything. If I just talked about my . . . new shoes all the time I'm sure you'd get fed up.

Laura It's New Year's Eve!

Rebecca You can't compare a child to a pair of shoes.

Kate I didn't mean it like that.

Laura Please don't argue.

Rebecca You just don't understand, do you? Of course you don't.

Daniel That's enough now.

Rebecca These are children we're talking about, not something you go and buy down the supermarket.

Kate That's not what I . . .

Rebecca They're not an accessory or a commodity.

Laura Why don't we play a game?

Rebecca I suppose if that's all you've got, what else can you talk about?

Kate Will you stop going on?

Rebecca We're talking about something no amount of money could buy.

Kate Well, that's not strictly true.

Rebecca What?

Kate I thought you had IVF. Didn't you pay for that?

Daniel Kate.

Rebecca I don't know why I fuckin' came here.

Kate Neither do I.

Laura Why are you fighting?

Daniel I think we all need to calm down.

Rebecca I feel sorry for you. I really do. That you haven't got children and you probably never will. You'll never understand the love I feel for my children. And the love they feel for me. It's unlike anything else. The best thing that ever happened to me. Maybe you shouldn't have got rid of Carl's baby all those years ago. Then you'd understand. How old would he, she, be now? Sixteen? A teenager.

Kate is stunned into silence. Pause. Ben and Carl come through.

Carl What's all the noise?

Laura Ben, will you make them stop? They're arguing. I don't know why they're arguing.

Ben I need some fresh air.

Ben heads to the front door and opens it. Laura joins him at the door.

Laura Please, Ben, please . . .

Ben What the fuck are you whingeing about now?

Laura Baby?

Ben All you've done is whinge, moan and cry the whole time you've been here. I don't know why I fuckin' brought you.

Laura doesn't know what to do. She turns and runs out of the open door and disappears into the darkness.

Carl Oh, great.

Ben I'm not going after her.

Daniel Someone's got to, she's been terrified of what's out there all night.

Ben (*half quiet, to Carl*) Pass us the . . .

Kate (*to Rebecca*) You think you've got it all, don't you? The perfect life. Looking down on the rest of us. Like we're a load of failures.

Carl is caught between Ben and trying to hear what Kate and Rebecca are saying.

Ben Go on.

Carl No, shush.

Kate Maybe it's about time you knew what was really going on.

Rebecca What the hell does that mean?

Kate That it's not all perfect.

Rebecca What?

Ben Pass us it.

Kate Carl.

Rebecca Carl? What's Carl got to do with anything?

Ben Just give us it and I'll . . .

Carl Will you shut up for a minute!

Carl looks over to Kate and Rebecca.

Rebecca What's she going on about?

Carl looks down at the floor. Pause.

Kate Carl.

Rebecca What is this?

Kate Tell her.

Carl Leave it.

Kate Now's your chance.

Carl . . .

Rebecca Tell me, tell me what?

Carl Nothing.

Rebecca No, Kate wants you to tell me something. Come on, Carl.

Carl Now's not the . . .

Kate If you're not going to say anything, then . . .

Carl Kate.

Kate I think you should know . . .

Carl Kate! There's *nothing* to say.

Rebecca I'd like to hear your big news. What is it?

Carl It's late, we've all had too much of everything.

Kate But . . .

Carl Too much has been said already.

He grabs Rebecca's arm and tries to take her off to bed.

Rebecca No.

Carl Let's call it a night.

Rebecca No, I'm not . . .

Carl I don't know what Kate's talking about and I don't want to know. I don't want to hear another word.

Rebecca Carl . . .

Carl You're going to do as you're told for once.

Rebecca Let go of my . . .

Carl tries to drag Rebecca off but she pushes him away and moves over the other side of the room.

I'm not going anywhere till I hear what this is all about. Come on then, Kate.

Pause. All eyes on Kate. She doesn't know what to do.

We're all waiting to hear.

Daniel I think . . .

Rebecca Shush. What's the story, Kate? What's this big announcement?

Kate I . . .

Rebecca Yes.

Carl Kate.

Kate The thing is . . .

Carl Kate.

Rebecca (*to Carl*) Is there something going on between you two?

Carl . . .

Rebecca Is that it?

Carl . . .

Rebecca That's what it is.

Kate turns to Carl.

Kate Carl?

Kate and Rebecca both wait for an answer. Pause.

Carl No, Rebecca . . . you're wrong. There's nothing going on between me and Kate.

Rebecca No?

Carl No.

Rebecca turns to Kate.

Rebecca Kate?

Kate . . .

Rebecca Did you have something to say?

Kate looks at Carl. She can't say it.

Kate?

Kate No.

Rebecca No?

Kate No, there's nothing. Carl's right, there's nothing going on between us.

Rebecca Then what was it . . . ?

Kate Forget it.

Rebecca No, no. You said . . .

Kate I said forget it, leave it, just leave it, Rebecca.

Carl (*to Rebecca*) Satisfied? You had enough now?

> *Carl takes Rebecca's arm and drags her off.*
> *Kate stands frozen in the middle of the room.*
> *Pause.*
> *Daniel looks out towards the open door. It starts to rain.*

Daniel I think you should go and look for your fiancée.

Ben Yeah?

Daniel Yes.

> *Ben looks out.*

Ben Great, it's pissing down. (*He steps out.*) Laura!

> *He closes the door behind him. Kate and Daniel are left alone.*

Daniel What the fuck?

Kate How did I end up here? How did I end up putting everything on to him?

> *Pause.*

Daniel No?

> *Pause.*

You and Carl?

> *Kate doesn't answer.*

Have you been having an affair with him?

Kate It's not an affair.

Daniel What is it then?

Kate . . .

Daniel How long . . . ?

Kate Only a few months.

She looks down at the floor. Pause.

He said he loved me. He was going to leave her.

Daniel Oh my God.

Kate What was I thinking? I'd convinced myself it was a mistake us splitting up all those years ago. That he was 'the one'.

Daniel Oh shit.

Kate He was the answer. Everything was going to be alright. I really believed him. I even thought we'd have kids together.

Daniel I thought you'd 'made peace' with that.

Pause.

So what was going to happen while you were here?

Kate doesn't answer.

That's why you were pissed off she was here. With no Rebecca, were you and him going to be sneaking along corridors at night? Is that what this weekend was all about?

Kate No.

Daniel Where did we fit in to this? Were we the cover story?

Kate It wasn't like that.

Daniel You created this whole thing, just so you could be together.

Kate No, no . . .

Daniel Well, how was it going to work? How was your spiritual retreat going to work if you were spending the whole time banging Carl?

Kate That's not how it was. We were all coming away long before anything happened between me and him. We only . . . in the last month or two . . . I told him not to come. I wanted to cancel it, call it off but he said do it. It'll be fun. It'll be a chance for us to be together.

Daniel It's all his fault, isn't it?

Kate I know it's not. I shouldn't have listened to him . . . at all. How did I . . . He was miserable with Rebecca. And he was there for me after Matthew and my mum . . .

Daniel Is that 'cause I wasn't? Is it my fault now?

Kate Stop it, Daniel.

Daniel And there's you lecturing me about Adam. Telling me to send him home.

Kate That was different.

Daniel Yeah, what you've been doing is much more fucked-up.

Kate I should have left it in the past.

Daniel D'you think?

Kate I don't know what I'm doing.

Daniel I bet you told Adam to go, didn't you.

Kate No.

Daniel When your little love nest doesn't work out you think you'll break mine up too.

Kate I wouldn't do that.

Daniel You thought he was some stupid little kid.

Kate I just thought . . .

Daniel It didn't make any sense. Him just leaving like that.

Kate You've got to believe me. I didn't say anything.

Daniel You can't bear to see anyone else happy.

Kate Daniel, he went because you'd been leading him on. He came here for a shag and you just wanted to talk and hug.

Daniel is silent. Pause.

I shouldn't have said that.

Daniel Probably not.

Kate I'm sorry.

Daniel For which bit? What is going on in your head?

Kate can't answer.

I'm going to bed.

Kate Don't go now, leaving it like this.

Daniel Goodnight.

Kate No, no . . . Daniel.

Daniel heads off towards the bedrooms.
Ben comes back in.

Ben No sign of her.

Daniel D'you think she'll have run off somewhere?

Ben She'll come back. It's pitch black and raining. I can't see a thing.

Daniel But she's petrified of it out there. We should go and look for her.

Ben But look at it.

The rain batters down outside.

Kate Shall I come?

Daniel No. You stay here.

Ben We'll need . . .

Ben and Daniel go off to the kitchen.
Kate is left alone. She breathes deeply, trying to keep herself together. Pause.
She can hear raised voices. She goes over to the doorway leading to the bedrooms. Carl and Rebecca are arguing. She can't make out what they are saying. She listens.
Ben and Daniel come back through with their coats on.

See you in a minute.

They both go out and put their hoods up.

You go that way and I'll . . .

Daniel I think we should stick together.

Ben closes the door behind them.

(*Off.*) Laura!

Kate listens a moment longer to Carl and Rebecca arguing. A crash comes from inside their room. Kate moves away; she doesn't want to hear any more.
She goes to make herself a drink but the bottles she tries are all empty. She goes through to the kitchen.
The faint distant arguing continues from Carl and Rebecca's room. Then stops suddenly. Then Rebecca starts sobbing.

Laura pushes open the front door. She's drenched, her dressing-up clothes are covered in mud and she's shaking. Her make-up runs down her face. She looks half crazed. She comes into the empty room, leaving the front door wide open. The rain is battering down outside.

She looks round the room, not sure what to do. Pause. She then swiftly goes over to the drinks table and discovers all the bottles are empty too. She looks round for something else. She goes over to the dining table and drinks the dregs of someone's left-over wine. She then picks up the large knife that was used to cut the chocolate cake. She holds it strong in front of her like a weapon, like she's going to stab someone with it.

She's not sure where to go. She looks towards the kitchen and moves to go through, but stops at the door. She turns swiftly and heads across the room towards the bedrooms. She stops abruptly in the middle of the room and thinks.

Kate comes through the kitchen doorway, opening a bottle of wine. Laura doesn't hear. Kate sees Laura. Kate is about to speak but she's curious as to what Laura's doing. Laura's unaware of Kate as she suddenly turns the knife on herself and slashes her left wrist diagonally. Blood spurts up from the wound and she collapses onto the floor.

As she does this Kate lets out a scream.

Kate No!

Kate throws the bottle and opener to one side and rushes over to Laura. She's not sure what to do but quickly grabs a cream-coloured sweater off the sofa and goes to wrap it round the wound. Blood is pumping out everywhere. It's all too much.

Oh God. Oh God.

She quickly wraps the sweater round Laura's arm and presses down on it. Laura looks at Kate glassy-eyed. She smiles at Kate.

You're going to be alright.

She wraps more sweater round the wound as it turns red with the blood.

Carl! Rebecca! Come here . . .

Kate goes behind Laura and holds her in her arms. She presses down on the wound with one hand, it's not enough. She presses down with both hands as she's getting covered in blood herself.

(*To Laura.*) I don't know what I'm doing . . . I think this is what you do.

Laura smiles at her.

Laura Shush.

She closes her eyes.

Kate No, no, stay with me.

Kate shakes Laura's head to keep her awake. Laura opens her eyes.

Carl! Come here, please, someone . . .

Laura It's alright . . .

She closes her eyes again

Kate No, it's not.

Kate shakes her to keep her awake.
Carl looks round the doorway.

Carl What's . . . (*He sees what's going on.*) What . . .

Kate You've got to help me I don't know what I'm doing.

Carl Rebecca! Come here quick.

Rebecca (*off*) Fuck off, Carl.

Carl Just come here now, you stupid bitch. It's an emergency! (*To Kate.*) All I know is you've got to keep the pressure on.

Kate I'm doing that. Get me some towels or something.

Carl runs off to the bathroom. Rebecca appears at the door.

Rebecca What the . . . Oh my . . . What . . . ?

Kate She . . .

Rebecca sees the knife on the floor.

Rebecca She . . . ? Oh fuckin' hell.

Kate nods and starts crying.

Kate I don't know what . . .

Rebecca joins Kate on the other side of Laura.

Rebecca It's alright. You're doing the right thing. Keep your hands clamped tight. You've done really well. Lift up her arm. Elevate it above the heart.

Carl comes back with various towels and hands them to Rebecca. She uses the towels; she clearly knows what she's doing. Laura fades a bit.

Stay with us, Laura. You're going to be alright. (*To Carl.*) Phone an ambulance.

Carl But there's no signal.

Rebecca I got one outside.

Carl Shouldn't we take her ourselves?

Rebecca Look at the state of us. Take my phone. Go straight ahead, through the bushes and there was a hill there.

Carl runs out towards the bedrooms to get the phone.

Where were you when . . .

Kate I'd just come in . . . And she . . . I saw her do it . . .

Rebecca Oh God . . . (*To Laura.*) Let's dry you off a bit.

Rebecca dries her with the towels. Carl comes back in with Rebecca's phone.

Carl Which way?

Rebecca Just run until you get a signal.

Carl What should I say?

Rebecca What d'you think? We need a fuckin' ambulance here now. Quick.

Kate The Old Priory, they'll know where it is.

Carl runs out into the rain.
   Kate, Rebecca and Laura are left alone.

What should we do?

Rebecca Just wait. We've got to try and keep her calm. Don't want her going into shock.

Laura fades. Rebecca shakes her. Pause.

Carl's getting you an ambulance. You're going to be alright.

Laura You don't need to . . . I'm fine.

Laura fades again.

Kate Stay with us. It's me and Rebecca here. We're here for you.

Rebecca You know who we are, don't you?

Kate You still with us?

Laura Kate. Rebecca.

118

Kate That's right.

Rebecca looks at Kate. Kate looks back at her. An awkward moment. A moment of understanding between them. Pause.

Laura I don't understand.

Kate What don't you understand?

Laura I thought you were friends.

Rebecca We are.

Kate We've known each other for years.

Laura No, no . . . I thought you were all so wonderful. I really did.

She closes her eyes.
Blackout.

SCENE TWO

The next day. The room is tidied and clean. Everything cleared away. Bright sunlight streams in through the windows.

Kate comes in from the bedrooms. She's dressed casually. She takes in the room, slightly disorientated. She looks over at the spot where Laura was last night. It doesn't seem real.

A busy Rebecca wearing big dark glasses comes on with a cloth. She cleans the dining table.

Kate Oh.

Rebecca Morning.

Kate You shouldn't have.

Rebecca The least I could do.

Kate It almost looks like nothing happened.

Rebecca There's coffee through there.

Kate Thanks.

Rebecca continues to clean. Pause.

Have you slept?

Rebecca I've had a couple of hours. I don't know about Carl. He's still off his face.

Kate I couldn't sleep.

Rebecca finishes wiping the table and tidies the cushions on the sofa.

You don't need to do that.

Rebecca Nearly done.

She picks up a book on the side.

Has someone been reading the Bible?

Kate I was just . . . It's one of the books here . . .

Rebecca puts it back on the bookshelf with other books.

About last night . . .

Rebecca Less said the better.

Kate I just . . .

Rebecca I don't think there's anything to say. Do you?

Kate Well . . .

Rebecca stops for a second. She looks at Kate.

After what happened, everything that was said seems . . .

Rebecca Kate. I don't want to talk about it.

Rebecca finishes tidying and disappears through to the bedrooms.

Kate is restless. She's unsure what to do. She takes in the room.
Rebecca comes through carrying her overnight bag. Kate moves away from the door.

Kate You're leaving?

Rebecca I think it's best.

Carl comes through with his bag.

Carl We'd like to stay longer . . .

Rebecca No, we wouldn't.

Rebecca walks to the door and opens it wide. She stops in the open doorway.

Goodbye, Kate. We'll sort out any money we owe you. (*To Carl.*) Do you want to say your goodbyes?

Rebecca waits in the doorway but looks out. Pause.

Carl I feel like shit.

Kate You look it.

Carl Thanks.

Neither of them knows what to say. Pause.
Rebecca coughs at the door.

Kate You'd better go.

Carl Listen . . .

Kate It's fine.

Carl You know . . .

Kate Please don't say anything else.

Carl gives Kate an awkward kiss on the cheek.
Rebecca looks round but tries to disguise it as fixing her hair.

Carl (*quiet*) Sorry.

Rebecca can't quite hear.
    Kate and Carl break apart. Rebecca walks out of the door and down the path to their car.
    Daniel comes through the doorway from the bedrooms. He's dressed very casually.

Daniel You off?

Carl Yeah, see ya, mate.

Carl gives Daniel a hug.

Daniel Where's Rebecca?

Carl Gone to the car.

Daniel I'll come and . . .

Carl I'd leave it.

Daniel Do you two . . .

Kate No. It's fine.

Carl I'd better . . . See ya, then.

Daniel See ya.

Carl looks at Kate. There's nothing else to say. He leaves. Daniel shuts the door behind him.
    An awkward pause. They both look at each other.

I need some coffee.

Daniel goes through to the kitchen. Kate is left alone. Pause.
    An exhausted-looking Ben opens the front door. He steps inside and closes the door behind him. Pause.

Kate So . . . how is she?

Ben She's . . . She's alright . . . Well, she's still alive.

Kate Oh, right.

Ben She'll be okay . . .

Kate They keeping her in?

Ben That's what they do. Keep an eye on her. In case she does it again . . .

Kate She said anything?

Ben She doesn't know what happened. She said she was helping herself to some cake and slipped. I sort of believed her until I phoned her dad to let him know and he said, 'Not again.' He's on his way to see her. Did you see . . .

Kate nods.

It wasn't an accident?

Kate shakes her head.
Pause.

Kate How are you?

Ben I'm . . . I'm . . . okay. Yeah, yeah. Good . . .

Kate Ben.

Ben It's a beautiful day out there.

Kate You know it's alright to not be okay.

Ben I . . .

He stands there like a little boy lost. She goes over to him and puts her arms round him. He holds her tightly and starts to sob.

Kate It's okay. It's okay. Let it out.

She holds him as he cries. Pause. He tries to get himself together.

Ben What was I . . .

Kate You weren't to know.

Ben Yeah, but . . . even before the whole . . . You know . . . I don't know what I should . . .

Kate It's okay. You don't need to decide anything now.

Pause.

Ben I'll get her stuff.

Ben goes off to the bedrooms. As he does, Daniel comes back through with a coffee.

Daniel Is that Ben?

Kate Yeah.

Daniel And?

Kate Laura's okay. She's alright.

Daniel God.

Pause.

I still can't . . .

Ben comes back on with all Laura's bags and his own small one. Ben and Daniel acknowledge each other.

Ben I'll take this stuff down . . .

Kate You don't have to do it straight away, do you?

Ben I'd rather get it done.

Daniel Is there anything . . . ?

Ben Thanks. It's . . .

Ben heads past Daniel. Daniel gives him a hug.

Daniel See ya.

Ben See ya.

Kate I'll give you a call later.

Ben I've got no . . . It's still . . . We'll speak.

He heads past Kate and gives her a kiss on the way.

Thank you.

Kate Keep in touch.

Ben makes his way out, carrying all the bags. Kate closes the door behind him. Kate and Daniel are left alone.

It's just us two, then.

Daniel What do we do now?

Kate You said you wanted the place to ourselves.

Daniel Shall we just go and pack?

Kate You want to go?

Daniel You can't want to stay.

Kate Yeah.

Daniel Oh no. Everything is saying we shouldn't be here. The universe is telling us to leave. The monks aren't happy.

Kate I want to stay.

Daniel You're on your own.

Kate Please.

Pause.

Daniel Why?

Kate Why not?

Pause.

I'm sorry.

Pause.

Can we start again?

Daniel sits down on the sofa.

Daniel What the hell are we going to do?

Kate Nothing. We don't have to do anything.

Kate joins him on the sofa.
Pause.

You know we used to joke about becoming smackheads because all you'd have on your list each day would be . . .

Daniel 'Get smack.'

Kate Yeah.

Daniel No worrying about how well you're doing, how you look, whether you smell of shit . . .

Kate Yeah.

Daniel So you're going to become a smackhead?

Kate No.

Pause. She thinks.

When I go back, I'm giving it all up.

Daniel You what?

Kate All the striving for some big thing. Having to prove myself. Waiting for some future time when I'm going to be happy. Tomorrow, next week, next year. This is it.

Daniel Oh God, I know.

Kate This is it and this is alright. Me and you here could be alright. Me teaching people to read and write. It's alright. This is it. This is it. This is it.

A face in a black hood appears at the window. It's not clear who it is.
Blackout.

End of play.